crosscurrents

VOLUME 73 : NUMBER 1 : MARCH 2023

SPECIAL ISSUE:
THE THEOLOGIES OF LAND

ARTICLES

1   Comparative Theology On and In Place:
An Introduction to the Special Issue
PAUL HEDGES

6   Mosaic Tiles: Comparative Theological Hermeneutics
and Christian-Jewish Dialogue About the Land
DOMENIK ACKERMANN

25   The Paradoxes of Place: Cultivating Particularity
and Planetarity Amid Climate Catastrophe
O'NEIL VAN HORN

42   The Batak-Christian Theology of Land:
Towards a Postcolonial Comparative Theology
HESRON H. SIHOMBING

64   Spirit(s) and the Land: A Comparative Theological
Exploration of Two Contemporary Indigenous Visions
MICHELLE VOSS ROBERTS

86   Conclusion
DOMENIK ACKERMANN

POETRY

88   For Jane, On Her Nephew's Birthday
SHANNON HARDWICK

89   For Jane, Three Days After Her Brother's Passing
SHANNON HARDWICK

CULTURAL CONNECTIONS

90 *Little Syria*, at the Brooklyn Academy of Music
    Reviewed by AYA NIMER

95 Rafael Lozano-Hemmer: Drawings in Smoke
    IRINA SHEYNFELD

101 Impossible Voyages: Wangechi Mutu at Storm King
    Reviewed by IRINA SHEYNFELD

108 CONTRIBUTORS

CrossCurrents (ISSN 0011-1953; online ISSN 1939-3881) connects the wisdom of the heart with the life of the mind and the experiences of the body. The journal is operated through its parent organization, the Association for Public Religion and Intellectual Life (APRIL), an interreligious network of academics, activists, artists, and community leaders seeking to engage the many ways religion meets the public. Contributions to the journal exist at the nexus of religion, education, the arts, and social justice. The journal is published quarterly on behalf of the Association for Public Religion and Intellectual Life by the University of North Carolina Press.

The Association for Public Religion and Intellectual Life (formerly ARIL) is a global network of leaders, scholars, and social change agents who explore religious life, engage in intellectual inquiry, and lead ethical action in the world today. Their primary objective, especially through annual summer colloquia, the online magazine *The Commons*, and the scholarly *CrossCurrents* journal, is to bring together leading voices of our time to advocate for justice and to examine global spiritual and interreligious currents in both historical and contemporary perspectives.

Information for subscribers: Institutional print-only subscriptions are available for $250/annually. Institutional digital ($250) and digital/print ($300) subscriptions are available through Project MUSE.

A membership to APRIL includes access to *CrossCurrents* starting with Volume 58, 2008, though our partners at Project MUSE, monthly newsletters, early access to summer colloquium themes, a 40% discount on UNC Press books, and more. Membership rates are listed below:
    Regular Membership with Digital Subscription: $55
    Seminary or Student Membership with Digital Subscription: $50
    Regular Membership with Print and Digital Subscription: $95
    Seminary or Student Membership with Print and Digital Subscription: $90

We have a partnership with Duke University Press (DUP) for membership fulfillment and subscriptions. Agencies are eligible for a discount on the institutional rate. If you have questions about an existing subscription or membership please contact DUP Journals Services:
    Email subscriptions@dukeupress.edu
    Phone toll-free in the US and Canada (888) 651-0122
    Phone (919) 688-5134
    Duke University Press Journal Services, Box 90660, Durham, NC 27708

Postmaster: Send all address changes to UNC Press, c/o Duke University Journal Services, 905 W. Main St. Ste 18-B, Durham, NC 27701.

© 2023 Association for Public Religion and Intellectual Life. All rights reserved.
For more information about APRIL and *CrossCurrents*, visit https://www.aprilonline.org/

EDITOR

S. Brent Rodriguez-Plate
  Hamilton College, USA

CULTURAL CONNECTIONS EDITORS

Rosalind Hinton
  Independent scholar, USA
Hussein Rashid
  Independent scholar, USA

ASSOCIATE EDITORS

Amanullah de Sondy
  University College Cork, Ireland
Timothy K. Beal
  Case Western Reserve, USA
Melanie Barbato
  University of Münster, Germany

EDITORIAL BOARD

Fatimah Ashrif
  Rumi's Circle; Muslim Institute, UK
Julia Watts Belser
  Georgetown University, USA
Joy Bostic
  Case Western Reserve, USA
Cláudio Carvalhaes
  Union Seminary, USA
Judy Chen
  *Buddhist Council of NY
  and the American Buddhist
  Confederation, Canada*
Robbie B. H. Goh
  *National University Singapore,
  Singapore*
Henry Goldschmidt
  Interfaith Center of New York, USA
Nikky-Guninder Singh
  Colby College, USA
Scott Holland
  Bethany Seminary, USA
Jonathan Homrighausen
  Duke University
Erling Hope
  Artist, USA
Amir Hussain
  Loyola Maymount University, USA
Robert P. Jones
  *Public Religion Research Institute,
  USA*
Björn Krondorfer
  Northern Arizona University, USA
J. Shawn Landres
  *Jumpstart Labs, Santa Monica,
  USA*
Laura Levitt
  Temple University, USA
Peter Manseau
  Smithsonian Institution, USA
Andrea Miller
  Writer, Editor at Lion's Roar
Shabana Mir
  American Islamic College, USA

Jolyon Mitchell
  University of Edinburgh, UK
Diane L. Moore
  Harvard University, USA
Harold Morales
  Morgan State University, USA
Vanessa Ochs
  University of Virginia, USA
Laurie L. Patton
  Middlebury College, USA
Daria Pezzoli-Olgiati
  *Ludwig Maximilian University,
  Germany*
Kathryn Reklis
  Fordham University, USA
Christian Scharen
  St. Lydia's Church, Brooklyn, USA
Randall Styers
  *University of North Carolina,
  Chapel Hill, USA*
Kayla Renée Wheeler
  Xavier University, USA
Pamela Winfield
  Elon University, USA
Homayra Ziad
  Johns Hopkins University, USA

APRIL BOARD OF DIRECTORS

PRESIDENT
Stephanie Mitchem
VICE-PRESIDENT
Björn Krondorfer
SECRETARY
Pamela Winfield
TREASURER
Judy Chen
EXECUTIVE DIRECTOR
S. Brent Rodriguez-Plate
Julia Watts Belser
Jonah Boyarin
Shabana Mir
Randall G. Styers
Sofia Ali-Khan

PUBLISHING WITH *CROSSCURRENTS*

Articles: Each issue includes 4-8 main essays, generally on a theme, though we will also publish unsolicited submissions. If you have questions or are interested in submitting an article for review, please contact the editor, Brent Rodriguez-Plate, splate@hamilton.edu

Cultural Connections: This section includes book reviews as well as reviews of film, television, museum exhibitions, and any place we see religion meeting the public. If you have an idea for a review of any current cultural works, please contact Hussein Rashid hr@husseinrashid.com and/or Rosalind Hinton rosalindhinton@mac.com

We will occasionally publish poetry and short creative writing.

PAUL HEDGES

COMPARATIVE THEOLOGY ON AND IN PLACE
An Introduction to the Special Issue

Since at least the 1990s, a new form of comparative theology has not just gained a foothold but has become an established part of the academic landscape. Unlike its namesake of the nineteenth century, it is not an apologetic venture but one based in an openness to genuine encounter and learning from those beyond the confines of the Christian heritage. Following most especially the seminal work of Francis X. Clooney, this new comparative theology has been a heavily textual tradition with in-depth reading of texts and commentaries.[1] Mastery of several languages and textual traditions has been the *sine qua non* for entry into and participation within the comparative theological game. But engagement with the religious Other has never been solely, or even primarily, a textual endeavor; people and traditions exist beyond and are far more than texts. Noting that exchanges at the interreligious level have always existed, what has been termed "theology" within a comparative mode has been the norm, not only in the Christian tradition but also globally, notwithstanding the problem of the modern usage of "religion" to denote discrete and distinct traditions.[2] The question, therefore, of whether comparative theology can extend beyond texts has been asked. Scholars such as Marianne Moyaert have emphasized through her work on inter-riting the possibility for comparative theology based around embodied and material aspects of tradition, especially liturgy.[3]

In this special issue, we explore this question in depth and seek an answer—if such a thing is still needed—to whether comparative theology can be done beyond the textual sphere. Here, the topic of land takes center stage, and we raise questions about embodiment, materiality, place, and belonging. Indeed, it helps show that in as far as written texts have a place it is only within a context, and that context is always located in place and time. In other words—arguably—place, space, land, embodiment, and materiality take precedence over the word, especially the word as inscribed within the pages of specific textual resources.

It is, perhaps, worth noting that the sheer physicality of the written text has become more obscure as we have moved through modernity and into today's post-/hyper-modernity (or whatever prefix, or lack thereof, one chooses). An inscription etched into a wall, or a vast stone stele placed within a courtyard, had an emplacement and physicality that was obvious. Even with the scroll, a specific ritualized form of opening, closing, and reading stressed materiality.[4] But as books moved into more accessible forms, whether in hard or soft binding, they became more portable and more divorced from place and land. Today, when we read them on a screen, anywhere, anyplace, and anytime, with texts of every era, location, and language but a few clicks away, the embodiment of written texts has become, almost literally, only a virtual reality; some books, of course, never exist as an actually tangible and handleable resource in our age. For a good number of journals that I have read and cited, some I have never even seen a physical copy of. This is not to say that place ever went away; we are always in a particular land and location when we read our online resources. Yet, for many years (some may say centuries), not simply texts, but a focus on ideas, and idealism, have dominated scholarly discourse. The material turn in academia, within which we may locate this special issue and its focus on land, is therefore part of more than a passing trend within comparative theology; it is part of a much larger—and arguably much needed—refocusing of scholarship on embodiment and materiality. Of course, an irony to this is that this commitment comes to us in written texts, and many of us will no doubt engage it as though disembodied and dislocated, reading about it on our isolated virtual platforms. I sit on a different continent from the editors and authors, and we have only communicated virtually about the importance of land and being in place! But as I write this, I see, perhaps, the premature emerging of spring in yellow flowers budding forth. I hear snatches of bird song and see the still bare branches of the trees as they emerge from winter. Being temporarily relocated from my home of eight years in Singapore to a college in Cambridge, I am very aware of my location. To the reader, therefore, I offer these words: as you read these papers, do not think about land, embodiment, and materiality as mere ideas to refresh academia as-it-was. How does your being-in-the-world, your locatedness, your embodied materiality, affect your reading, your reception, your engagement with the text?

Turning to the four papers, Domenik Ackermann's article, "Mosaic Tiles" deals with land as it exists in the encounter between Jewish and Christian traditions. Questions about what Israel means in Jewish and Christian readings of biblical texts, and of course the stark, political, and physical reality of the State of Israel play into this mix. Arguing for hermeneutical openness and humility, established values in comparative theological work, Ackermann acknowledges that the aim would not be to "fix" this; as though doing so were the work of interreligious dialogue or comparative theology. Rather, he raises a more open question about the potentialities of applying the virtues of comparative theological work to encounters and discussions around the Land of Israel, in its many and varied meanings. His essay is more focused on methods and questions that need to be asked, rather than fixed answers or showing the results of such an exercise.

Next, O'Neil Van Horn takes a different route, delving into negative theology and deconstruction. This may seem to be the opposite of emplacement and location, but at the risk of us being "undone" by the turns he takes, Van Horn suggests—via the works of Gregory of Nyssa and Catherine Keller—that we are pointed towards the paradox of all places being only ever processes of becoming (and he notes in passing what soil science may tell us about this) and being here only because they are not there. In other words, there is a paradox that emplacement is not being in a fixed place but in somewhere interconnected. As such, an interreligious encounter or comparative theological endeavor, he argues, is based not on any foundation, despite the necessity of focus on the regional and particular, but in the pluriform and interconnectedness that underlies our sense of religion, place, or homeland.

The following paper by Hesron H. Sihombing locates itself very particularly in relation to the Batak people (specifically the Batak Toba) of Indonesia as a basis for its theorizing. Sihombing brings together post/decolonial theory and spatial theory to provide conceptual lenses which are then brought into conversation with Batak ways of being, stressing that in such a context comparative theology must wrestle with the inevitable hybridity of religions; though speaking of "religion" itself is inadequate as culture, politics, economics, and so on are all embedded in Batak thought, and the term *adat*, roughly custom, is introduced. By separating *adat* and religion, it is noted that European missionaries divorced their notion of "salvation" from indigenous concepts of land and rejected the Goddess of the Land and local spirits of place. Meanwhile, economically, politically, and ecologically, the Batak people's land was taken from them and made into plantations with a rationale of mass production; (neo)colonization cannot simply be thought of as ideas. In light of the power imbalance, Sihombing calls for a "comparative reflectivity" that does not simply compare texts and concepts, but looks at the lived tradition. This paper also usefully challenges comparative theology to pay more attention to indigenous traditions, noting complexities in this engagement.

This focus is kept by Michelle Voss Roberts, who looks to indigenous traditions to engage in comparative theology around land. That both Sihombing's and Voss Roberts's papers on comparative theology and land engage indigenous traditions should not surprise us, because for many such groups their connection to place and land remains strong and is central to how they do "religion." Voss Roberts notes something true for (almost) all Western (comparative) theologians, though speaking for herself, when she states that land "escaped my categories . . . in ways I cannot quite comprehend." She also suggests that Western theologians "want a lesson to take away, without transforming our understanding of reality" when engaging what land means to indigenous traditions. Voss Roberts lets indigenous scholars speak for themselves, focusing especially on Alf Dumont (from the Anishinaabe of present-day Canada) and Keneipfenuo Rüpreo Angami (from the Nagaland of present-day Northern India). She also speaks of the hybridity of religions, using the term creolization. Importantly, in referencing Dumont, Roberts notes that he does not "outline a theology of the land" but in his work "the land's agency appears in narrative form." This, I think is worth taking note of, for having correctly noted how indigenous thought on the land can exceed our categories, it may be too easy to try and construct a comparative theology of the land where it becomes the subject of our theology. But this may miss what we have to learn about the land's agency. This, in relation to my earlier comments, emphasizes the importance of what we may learn from these articles.

NOTES
1. The classic study remains Clooney, *Comparative Theology*.
2. These points are argued in Hedges, *Comparative Theology*.
3. Moyaert and Geldhof, eds. *Ritual Participation*.
4. See, among others, Watts, *Iconic Books and Texts*. On the material turn in the study of religion, see Hedges, *Understanding Religion*, Chapter 9 and Chapter 3

BIBLIOGRAPHY

Clooney, Francis X. *Comparative Theology: Deep Learning Across Religious Borders*, Chichester, UK: Wiley-Blackwell, 2010.

Hedges, Paul. *Comparative Theology: A Critical and Methodological Perspective*. Leiden: Brill, 2017.

———. *Understanding Religion: Theories and Methods for Studying Religiously Diverse Societies*. Berkeley: University of California Press, 2021.

Moyaert, Marianne, and Joris Geldhof, eds., *Ritual Participation and Interreligious Dialogue Boundaries, Transgressions and Innovations*. London: Bloomsbury, 2015.

Watts, James W., ed. *Iconic Books and Texts*. Sheffield, UK: Equinox, 2013.

DOMENIK ACKERMANN

MOSAIC TILES
Comparative Theological Hermeneutics
and Christian-Jewish Dialogue About the Land

The first time I encountered the complexity of the situation surrounding the Land of Israel/Palestine was during my studies in Beirut, Lebanon. Having been raised in Germany in a school system committed to repairing the great harm done by my ancestors to many millions of Jewish people, the importance of a place of safety for the Jewish people was unquestionable in my mind. I had listened to the personal stories of Holocaust survivors and read the diaries of victims of the Shoah. However, my encounter with Lebanese Christians, Palestinian Christians, and Muslims, and the harsh rhetoric against the policies of the State of Israel have shown me an alternative narrative. Likewise, I attended to the personal stories of people who were not able to go back to the towns their parents and grandparents had grown up in the Land. In 2019, I had yet another important study abroad in Jerusalem, which showed me yet another story of the richness, the love, and the conflict surrounding the Land.[1]

Upon my return from my various studies, I could not help but describe the stories that I had heard and listened to as mosaic tiles of a larger picture. The Land has been a polarizing topic in attempted dialogues between Jews and Christians—and within the context of all the Abrahamic traditions around Israel, Palestine, and the Occupied Territories. The various publications and attempts to discuss issues around the contested land present a kaleidoscope of ideas and responses, from liberation theologies to Zionism(s).[2] Some are even confident that they offer a solution for the conflict. Interreligious dialogue between Christians and Jews on this issue has been hampered by walls of opinion that prevent sincere engagement with the topic. This article addresses some of the challenges that occur due to the diversity of theologies of the Land within the context of Jewish-Christian dialogue, particularly from a mainline Protestant point of view. I argue that a comparative theological approach of humility and hermeneutic openness can be an alternative to the attempts made in the past, both academically and in the practice of Jewish-Christian dialogue, to recognize the variety and often opposing opinions in discussions about the Land.

To be sure, the conflict around the land inhabited by citizens of the State of Israel and Palestine is itself a political one. Two cultural identities and three religious traditions (i.e., Islam, Judaism, and Christianity) claim the same right to live in this land, but only one of them has the political power to govern it. However, this political conflict radiates into the theological spheres in both Christianity and Judaism. One of the reasons is because the name *Israel* has a multi-layered meaning. Besides its reference to the State of Israel today, it biblically refers to the ground upon which that state is built and the cultural identity of a people. Within Jewish religious traditions in America, political views, when conflated with theological issues, cause differences within otherwise cohesive communities.

Furthermore, these meanings of Israel receive further interpretations and ideologies in both Jewish and Christian traditions. The trajectories within Protestantism are manifold, ranging from a theological Zionism similar to that espoused by some Jewish communities to a liberation theology approach, and each has its own theological arguments and practical implications.

As a clergy member in the United Church of Christ (UCC) who engages in Jewish-Christian dialogue with a comparative theological approach at both the academic and local church levels, I believe that comparative theological hermeneutics may be helpful in the dialogue between Jews and Christians about the Land. Thus, the purpose of this article is to outline an approach for religious bodies to dialogue between Christians and Jews within the North American context. This approach contains some hermeneutic keys of contemporary comparative theological work in the academic field. However, it is suitable for the practical work done within the settings of Jewish-Christian dialogue. To achieve this purpose, this article will unfold in three steps. First, it outlines what I would call "mosaic tiles" of ideologies around Israel that do not translate well into the ideologies of other dialogue partners. This section highlights that within the main factions of thought, there are layers of complexities.

The second step involves outlining some key characteristics of the hermeneutics of comparative theology, especially its emphasis on textuality, hermeneutic openness, and humility. I engage recent comparative theological approaches from Francis X. Clooney, Catherine Cornille, and Marianne Moyaert to highlight three hermeneutic approaches in comparative theology, which are con-text, hermeneutic openness, and humility. I believe these are vital for an interreligious conversation about the Land.

In the third and final step, I engage these three hermeneutic characteristics by applying them to the topic of the Land in Christian-Jewish dialogue. It is my hope to show that the engagement with the con-texts of the religious other with an approach of hermeneutic openness and an attitude of humility and empathy can nourish the dialogue between the two traditions. The outlined components ideally mean to be a practical orientation that leads to dialogue in both academic and non-academic contexts. Sincere engagement with the topic of the Land needs to leave room for the particularity of the different opinions and the openness also to be changed in one's own views. Finally, a search for narratives of the various positions may facilitate an attitude of humility and empathy, that is, imagining the other's experience of the topic as if it was our own.

A final note regarding the scope of this endeavor: The purpose of this article is not to find a solution to the political conflict about the Land, let alone any issue within this conflict. Additionally, I do not seek to create a pathway to "normalization." Rather, my intention here is merely to offer a hermeneutic framework for dialogue within the Jewish and Christian traditions about the political conflict.

A MOSAIC OF IDEOLOGIES ON THE LAND

The topic of the Land has long been contentious in the dialogue between Jews and Christians, both on an academic and an ecclesial level. Before going into detail about the issues that cause difficulties in the dialogue today, it is helpful to understand the roots of ideological thoughts around the Land. One can indeed say that these ideologies are multifaceted, like mosaic tiles. Due to the complexity of the issues, it is only possible to sketch the basic strands of thought around the Land of Israel. In a recent attempt to sketch such a spectrum in Christian theologies, Jesper Svartvik distinguishes between *Christian Zionism* and *Christian Palestinianism*, although he contends that one needs to think about these terms in the plural because within those categories, we find spectra of opinions, emphasizing the complexity around the topic of the Land.[3] For the purpose of this article, I will use the spectrum of these two ideologies, although more so as to highlight this divergence between the two ideologies in both religious traditions. This, I shall briefly illustrate four streams of thought by offering one representative of each thought.

Religious Zionism
In her recent contribution on the theologies of the Land from a Jewish perspective, Ruth Langer poignantly states that "Jewish theologies of Israel intertwine the concepts of peoplehood, land, and state into a complex matrix that for Jews is often self-evident or simply not probed."[4] It is a quite modern Western idea to separate those concepts. Jacob was renamed Israel, and likewise his descendants received the name Israel, relating to the tribes of Israel, which is first mentioned in Gen. 49:16–28. In the book of Exodus, Israel, then is referred to as the people of Israel (Exod. 11:10). In Jewish understanding, God's covenant with the people of Israel includes the giving of the Land. Hence, it is according to Jewish understanding that God wishes for the people of Israel to live in the land that God promised them: The Land of Israel.[5] Until today, Jewish theology, which expresses itself mostly in Jewish liturgical practice, has been centered around this Land.

Likewise, in messianic Judaism, the Land becomes of central importance. Among the many voices in this mosaic of understandings, the most notable representative at the beginning of the twentieth century was Abraham Isaac Kook (1865–1935), a mystic Jew from Eastern Europe who lived in Palestine. He represents a messianic Judaism that is concerned with living a Jewish life with the imminent expectation of the coming of the Messiah:

> "Redemption is continuous. The Redemption from Egypt and the Final Redemption are part of the same process, "of the mighty hand and outstretched arm," which began in Egypt and is evident in all of history . . . The spirit of Israel is attuned to the hum of the redemptive process, to the sound waves of its labors which will end only with the coming of the days of the Messiah."[6]

According to Kook, full redemption requires Jews to unite with body, soul, and land. Kook's concern was that Jewish people in the diaspora do not receive "real and organic holiness" at the end of days if they did not first return to the Land.[7] Thus, living a life of purity was essential for messianic Jews. Relatedly, in his work *Orot,* Kook emphasized the inseparability of the Land of Israel and the "soul" of the Jewish people.[8] A Jew, Kook asserts, cannot thrive and be devoted "to his own ideas, sentiments, and imagination in the diaspora as he can in Eretz Israel," which causes pure thinking and a closer understanding of truth.[9] Consequently, every Jew should be longing to be in the Land that God gave the Jewish people.

With Kook's holistic understanding of peoplehood, nationhood, and land, his critique of secular Zionism is unsurprising. Secular Zionists, Kook believed, are erroneous in their belief that the Jewish spirit can be separated from the spirit of God. Instead, nationhood, Land, and the divine covenant between God and Israel can only be thought of together.[10]

On the Christian side, we also find Zionist movements, also referred to as Christian Zionism. Its origins lie in the aftermath of the Protestant Reformation, when the translation of the Bible into the vernacular revealed the unique relationship between God and the Jews. Most notably, Puritans in England and the Netherlands expressed the centrality of the Jewish people to God and God's divine providence. Thus, voices arose in England to repeal the Edict of Expulsion (1290) against the Jewish people and, separately, to request Jews to be transported back to their homeland in Palestine.[11]

However, the term "Christian Zionism" is a more recent invention. In his book *Evangelicals and Israel*, Stephen Spector argues that, even though the term appeared in the nineteenth and even in the early in the twentieth century, it only gained recognition in the 1990s.[12] The basic understanding within Christian Zionism is that its ideology refers to Christians who support the State of Israel as the homeland of the Jewish people. One early twentieth century representative of this movement was William Blackstone, who urged President Benjamin Harrison to restore Palestine as the homeland for the Jewish people.[13] It seems that there are two broad approaches of Christian Zionism today. First, many Christian Zionists after Blackstone and until today reference Gen. 12:3, "I will bless those who bless you, and the one who curses you I will curse; and in you all the families of the earth shall be blessed" (NRSV) as their reason to support the State of Israel. The support of Israel becomes the premise of Gen. 12:3 that one receives a blessing when one treats blessed people well. According to Spector most Christian Zionists believe that the United States has been blessed due to its loyalty to the Jewish people. Consequently, it is also commonly believed that not treating Jews well can cause a curse upon oneself, as well.[14]

The other broad approach of Zionism is dispensationalist theology, which is a theology that can be traced back to John Nelson Darby. Dispensationalist theology holds that today we live in the last "dispensation" of the prophecies revealed in the biblical book of Revelation. According to this belief, we are living at the end of times, in which the second coming of the Messiah is near. During these end times, God will initiate a "rapture" or transport of all Christian believers away from earth to initiate a time of trial ("tribulation"). Then, 144,000 Jews would be converted to Christianity to proselytize all non-believers to Christianity.[15]

Secular Zionism
In her outline on Jewish ideas about the Land, Langer sketches the historical development of Jewish self-understanding and outlines how, in the aftermath of the French Revolution and Napoleon's emancipation of Jews in Europe, Jews understood Judaism and Jewishness to be matters of religion rather than nationality.[16] While, according to Langer, this self-identification did not find acceptance among all Jewish people in Europe, it did influence scholarly discussion, and ultimately, the rise of the idea of non-religious or secular Zionism. The roots of these Zionist ideologies lie in nineteenth-century Europe. The most famous representative of non-religious Zionism is Theodor Herzl. Although not the creator of the term Zionism, he was one of the most fervent advocates for a Jewish State in the territory of Palestine.[17] Concerned about the general status of Jews in Europe, Herzl claims that such a state would offer the only way for Jews to have a place of safety. Notably, in *The Jewish State* (1896), Herzl envisions the restoration of a Jewish State.[18] Herzl claims that only such a state can protect Jews from increasing oppression, persecution, and antisemitism.[19] Until there is a Jewish State, Herzl writes, "I think we shall not be left in peace."[20] Interestingly, Herzl primarily refers to Jews as an ethnic group. However, he does reference religious language such as "next year in Jerusalem," a reference to the Passover Seder, which expresses the messianic hope to return from exile back to the Land. In his First Congress Address (1897) in Basel, Herzl emphasizes that his Zionist idea is not merely a concept referring to the return to a Jewish land but a "return to the Jewish fold."[21] Herzl recognizes that the Zionist movement created unity among liberal and conservative Jews. Overall, Herzl's ideas on a Jewish State are theoretical, visionary ideas. Although he indicates specific practical steps one should take to realize such an idea, such as an inquiry to the Ottoman Empire that occupied the territory at the time, Herzl himself clarified that he did not want to think about legal issues at the time. Instead, he was concerned with spreading the general idea of the restoration of a Jewish State.[22]

Liberation Theologies about the Land

Unlike most Zionist ideas, liberation theologies reflect a context after the establishment of the State of Israel, and are responses to the subsequent rising Israeli-Palestinian conflict, which resulted in Al-Nakba, or catastrophe, in 1948. There have been a set of important voices within this Palestinian liberation theology. Probably the first and most notable representative of this theology is Naim Ateek, an Episcopalian Palestinian priest. His book "Justice and only Justice: A Palestinian Theology of Liberation" (1989) rejects the Zionist ideas about the claim of the Land by Jews. Particularly, Ateek criticizes the Zionist interpretation of the Hebrew Bible as a place and homeland for Jews only.[23] Ateek offers an alternative reading of the meaning of the Land. For instance, Ateek refers to Ezekiel's Jerusalem Vision, particularly in Ezek. 47:21–23. Here, Ezekiel describes God's vision of the re-establishment of Jerusalem after the exile, including Israel's tribes. Ateek interprets Ezekiel's vision of Jerusalem as a place of greater inclusion.[24]

Throughout his work, Ateek's liberation theology offers a critique oriented toward a traditional view of Jewish theology as too focused on Jewish particularity in contrast to a Christian universal approach. Ateek believes that, basing their theology on a tribal understanding of God through the lens of the Hebrew Scriptures Jewish teachings emphasize the strict separation between Jews and Christians, which also manifests in the Jewish beliefs of the Land. Jews, Ateek emphasizes, consider the Land as in their only possession, and Palestinians are considered as aliens.[25] Overall, Ateek's approach of a Palestinian theology of liberation to advocate for the right of the Palestinian people to remain and live in the Land.[26] Another prominent voice within the context of Ateek's voice include the works of Mitri Raheb, whose work can be categorized more as contextual theology. Famously, his book I am a Palestinian Christian is a thoughtful presentation of Palestinian Identity within the political, real-life context of the conflict in the Land. Similar to Ateek, Raheb criticizes the Jewish theological claim of the promise of Land within the modern context. For instance, he contextualizes the biblical understandings of the borders of the land with modern-day understanding, saying that even in the Bible, the Land had never been a purely Jewish state.[27]

Also, within the Jewish discourse approaches to liberation theology emerged. Noteworthy here is the work of Marc H. Ellis, who initiated a turn toward the possibility of a Jewish liberation theology. Generally speaking, Ellis's approach on liberation is not focused on the specific issues on the land. However, it does play a role within this context in its particular application. Ellis's approach is a Jewish attempt to "liberate" Judaism from a generalistic view that Jewish people are those historically oppressed toward a view of Judaism as a religion of awareness and solidarity. Within this theology, Ellis addresses the conflict about the Land. If Jewish Liberation theology is one of solidarity with the oppressed, Ellis claims, it must also be one of solidarity with those oppressed in the context of the Israel-Palestine conflict.[28]

Mainline Protestantism
The main positions that I just outlined above are but mosaic tiles within their own ideological discourses. While they represent the main streams of thought, there are subgroups and nuances within those four branches. The ongoing political tensions between the State of Israel and the Palestinian territories reignited political theological debates within those groups, with some criticizing the political actions of the State of Israel in theological terms. These approaches largely reverberated in the mainline Protestant Churches, especially in the United States, for multiple reasons. One reason is that most large denominations have alliances and partnerships with church bodies in the Middle East, especially in Palestine. In return, they have drawn criticism from Jewish scholars who highlight that the approaches revert some of the progress made between Christian and Jews in dialogue with one another, highlighting a Christian return to stereotypical thinking about Jews. Most poignantly, Gregerman highlights the return of stereotypical thinking about Jewish Particularism versus Christian universalism, covenantal supersessionism, and the return of generalizing negativity against Jews.[29] Similarly, Christian churches, allied with Palestinian Christians and churches, raised critical voices against the attitude of the State of Israel toward Palestinians. These critiques caused hardened fronts.

After many years of eloquent silence among scholars and churches who engage in Christian-Jewish dialogue on the topic of the Land, theological critiques of the State of Israel have been renewed. In its resolution *Declaration for a Just Peace between Palestine and Israel* in June 2021, the United Church of Christ rejects "the use of Scripture to claim a divine right to the land as the rationale for Israel's illegal seizure and annexation of Palestinian land," as well as "any laws and legal procedures which are used by one race or religion or political entity to enshrine one people in a privileged legal position at the expense of another, including

Israel's apartheid system of laws and legal procedures." This resolution went so far as to use the theological language of declaring Israel's occupation of Palestine a sin.[30] More recently, the Presbyterian Church also declared Israel an apartheid state.[31] There is a need for dialogue among Christians and Jews about the Land, yet the recent developments seem to harden the frontlines.

COMPARATIVE THEOLOGICAL HERMENEUTICS: PATIENCE, OPENNESS, AND HUMILITY

The previous overview offers only a few among many mosaic tiles and fractions of ideologies around the Land. Each of them deserves a closer look at their theologies and their practice than I can offer here if one seeks to engage them in the practice of Jewish-Christian dialogue. However, as a Christian scholar who is concerned both about the political situation in the Land and the dialogue between Jews and Christians on this topic, I see it as necessary to reflect on how to approach an interreligious dialogue on the Land that respects and values the various mosaic tiles. In a climate of increased divisions and heightened aggressions in our society, we need to think over our approach to dialogue on this matter. My primary argument here is that a comparative theological approach of contextuality, hermeneutic openness and humility offers a unique path toward dialogical practice on the topic of the Land between Jews and Christians, especially within the context of the religious institutions in North America. In what follows, I will outline three vital aspects of doing comparative theology: the reading of the "text" of another religious tradition, hermeneutic openness, and an approach of humility.

Reading another tradition's "text"

The most traditional way of engaging in comparative theology happens through reading and engaging with texts in a comparative manner. However, unlike in the study of comparative religion, where scholars compare two texts merely for the sake of comparison, the comparative theological approach always seeks to find theological enrichment for one's tradition. For instance, in his book *Theology after Vedanta*, comparative theologian Francis X. Clooney outlines his method of practicing theology in dialogue with another tradition. Clooney emphasizes a focus on the classic texts one examines. Reading a text from a different tradition is the basis for relating it to one's own tradition. Clooney exemplifies this confessional approach, maintaining that comparative work is in its nature more exegetical and engaged with the text of a foreign tradition. Clooney asserts that he is "more attentive to how learning, writing, and true knowledge follow from patient reading."[32] The purpose of this exercise is to enlighten one's own religious tradition by reading the other tradition's text. The emphasis here is on learning about the other and the self by prioritizing deep reading over the questions of the larger picture. This learning can either confirm, rectify, or even enhance one's own view. Daniel Joslyn-Siemiatkoski's Christian commentary on the Mishnah Avot is another example of such comparative theological work.[33] It is a Christian commentary of a Jewish text that offers insights for Christians from the rabbinic text.

This understanding of reading another tradition's text can be applied to the practice of dialogue. However, real dialogue does not happen between texts but in written or oral conversation between humans of different traditions. In order to approach this idea of reading another tradition's text, one needs to broaden the interpretation of "text" toward an encounter with a con-text. In recent years, the understanding of textual work has been broadened. Marianne Moyaert argues poignantly that real interreligious dialogue is always a personal encounter. Instead of using the idea of comparing texts, Moyaert borrows from Paul Ricœur by talking about different "languages." Thus, in an interreligious encounter different languages come together, trying to understand each other. I should like to appropriate this understanding of language in combination of Clooney's understanding of working with another text because there are similarities between the reading of another text and a conversation with another's opinion. In an ideal situation, I am reading a text or am listening to the other in a dialogue so that I can understand the other's opinion. Similar to the text, the other's opinion is always embedded with a particular context. A clear understanding of the other involves my understanding of the other's con-"text."

Hermeneutic openness
When engaging with another tradition's text, any comparison will come to a new understanding, either about another tradition or one's own background. However, every such comparison needs to be based on two hermeneutic presuppositions: my knowing of my own standpoint, and my openness toward the viewpoint of the other. It requires the willingness to "transpos[e] oneself into the worldview and experience of the other, and [attempt] to understand oneself and one's own tradition

from that perspective."[34] Catherine Cornille argues that this approach, though, is also a complex interplay between my seeing myself through the other and seeing the other through myself.

The outcome of what Cornille calls "transposition" into the worldview of the other has multiple facets. In her book *Meaning and Method in Comparative Theology,* she highlights possible approaches of coming to a new understanding through comparative theological practice. One may be able to intensify or rectify one's own position. One may recover a lost understanding or reinterpret, or one may appropriate a new understanding from the other tradition. Finally, one may conclude that the reading of another tradition reaffirms one's own beliefs.[35] All of these learnings are possible, and sometimes multiple ways of learning may happen at the same time. Like the textual approach, this hermeneutic approach of how we come to a new understanding can also be applied to our dialogue attempts. For instance, in a mutual dialogue about the Land, a Christian party with a mainline Protestant focus and a conservative Jewish party with a Zionist focus may come to learn from each other. The Christian may learn about the multi-faceted meaning of Israel as a people, connected with God's promise of the Land. The Jewish parties may learn about their modern Christian view of the separation of state and religion. This may result in both parties coming to a new insight into the relationship between religion and politics.

However, for this learning to happen within dialogue, one needs to approach the dialogue with hermeneutic openness. Moyaert argues that such a dialogue may be successful only through hermeneutic openness. How do we attain an approach of hermeneutic openness? Similar to the textual approach, Moyaert explains that this approach to being exposed to the other is achieved in becoming vulnerable toward the other with the expectation that I potentially learn from the other and be immersed in the world of the other. In this state, one can go into meaningful dialogue. Moyaert, borrowing here again from Ricœur and George Lindbeck's cultural-linguistic theory by using his analogy of religion as a language, contends that no language can be fully translated into another without losing meaning.[36] Translating this point into the interreligious encounter, Moyaert emphasizes that genuine interreligious dialogue leaves room for particularity.[37] To be sure, there is a loss of meaning. However, this inability to translate all meaning also acknowledges diversity. The balance between understanding the other and what cannot be translated into one's own tradition is, Moyaert argues, a "fragile hermeneutical space" in which one needs to strike a balance between one's own opinion and the other's opinion.[38]

I believe a strength in this approach on hermeneutic openness lies within its emphasis on particularity of the other's context. Such a vulnerability requires all parties to leave room for the particularities of on another party's opinion. It may also require each party to be open to be changed by the experience of the dialogue. Traditional comparative theological approaches of inclusivism or pluralism always imply a judgment about the other's validity or correctness. Moyaert's approach actively tries to avoid such judgment in those encounters.

I may learn something new about my position through the lens of the other, and something new about the other that may enrich my own worldview. Similar to the textual approach on learning, this hermeneutic openness may result in the same types of learning about oneself and the other during the dialogue.

Humility

The comparative theological approach toward another religious tradition requires an attitude of humility. This humility has a variety of forms. In order to be open to the richness of the other's point of view and the possibility of learning about me or the other, there needs to be an acceptance that my own view may be incomplete. This awareness is a form of humility that is necessary for any interreligious engagement as well. Indeed, a dialogue without hermeneutic openness dissolves into apologetic claims of one's own opinions without the willingness to learn from one another.

Another form of humility not often directly brought into the conversation in comparative theology is the decentering one's own ideas. Kathryn Tanner's description of Christian identity is fruitful in conceptualizing this notion. Tanner describes that Christian identity is not established at its center but at its margins through the interaction with other traditions at the margins.[39] She relativizes the importance of one's self as always in conversation and relationships with other identities. Marc A. Krell interprets Tanner's viewpoint poignantly by stating that "religious uniqueness is not preserved within a boundary, but rather produced through cultural interaction at the boundary where theological statements are made."[40] Krell, then, continues to develop an idea in which theology should move away from theological approaches that center around themselves and focus instead on the interaction at the boundaries. One can describe this decentering as an approach of humility inasmuch as it involves the realization that one's identity is always interdependent on the neighbor. This approach stands in contrast to a method in which one considers one's own tradition or values as superior to another.

Approaching a text with humility likewise translates to the practice of interreligious dialogue. Genuine interreligious dialogue forms out of the willingness to learn from each other's religious traditions on particular topics of convergence. Even application-oriented dialogue with the more ethical goal of working on communal issues ultimately requires a form of humility in which one realizes that one needs the partner tradition to achieve a goal. It is a form of removing oneself from one's center.

CONCERNING JEWISH-CHRISTIAN DIALOGUE ABOUT THE LAND

Above, I have outlined what I called mosaic tiles in the landscape of ideologies about this geographic space that people call Israel or Palestine today. They all are pieces of a larger picture, a mosaic of ideas within themselves. However, these tiles may also be arranged into a larger picture by bringing them together. I argue that comparative theological hermeneutics has the potential to be fruitful for such an exercise. Suppose the hermeneutic approaches of textual encounter, openness, and humility in the comparative theological study apply to interreligious dialogue. In that case, they certainly also appertain to interreligious attempts to converse about the Land. However, how do we use the comparative theological approach to the dialogue about the Land between Jews and Christians?

The commitment to intertextuality becomes vital in dialogue when we consider each other's contexts, especially each other's stories. One can only understand these mosaic tiles within their own historical, theological, and biographical contexts. I propose approaching a conversation with each of these tiles within their respective mosaic by engaging with the stories behind the values they represent. For instance, Herzl's idea about a Jewish state derived from his biographical experience as part of an oppressed community in central Europe. Likewise, Ateek's liberation theology originates in his own experience of being a Christian Palestinian born and raised in the Land, having witnessed the wars after U.N. Resolution 181 in 1947 on the partition of the Land and the establishment of the State of Israel in 1948. The first attempt in an interreligious encounter may be listening to the personal stories, presenting all these mosaic tiles in their own context, and acknowledging these various experiences.

Suppose one wants to pursue further dialogue on the topic of the Land and try to understand each other in their commonalities and differences. In that case, the attitudes of hermeneutic openness and humility are vital for success. When listening to each other's personal stories, we need to open ourselves to these stories by allowing ourselves to transpose ourselves into the account of the other and viewing the story of the other through our own eyes, and perhaps even see our position from the other's perspective. What would a dialogic encounter look like between a Palestinian Christian who shares their personal story about living in Palestine with a Christian Zionist who practices genuine hermeneutic openness? Likewise, what would such an encounter look like between a Jew persecuted in Europe who dreams of refuge without oppression and a Palestinian who sees his position through the eyes of the other's encounter?

Finally, any interreligious dialogue about the Land needs to happen on the grounds of humility. In this context, we need to acknowledge the possibility that we may learn about another's views and that these views may enrich, rectify, or enhance our understanding of the Land. Perhaps, we can learn about the impact of our position on the other. However, true humility requires each party to take a step back and realize that a Jewish-Christian dialogue about the Land cannot "fix" the situation in the Land. An attitude by which such attempted conversations within the North American Christian context can and should resolve the conflict between Palestinians and Israelis is hegemonic. It resembles the colonial approaches when European and Western political administrations tried to find solutions that, ultimately, are factors that also caused the conflict. Instead, the conversations with one another may encourage us and each other to acknowledge differences and the still-existing tensions.

The work of the organization Parents Circle-Families Forum (PCFF) is an excellent example of context, hermeneutic openness, and humility. One of the chief programs of this organization is its Parallel Narrative Experience, which seeks to highlight different personal narratives from both Jewish and Palestinian sides through dialogue. The organization hosts two dialogue partners from opposing sides of the conflict, with their own biographies and contexts, and brings their stories into conversation. In other words, two mosaic tiles come together. PCFF states that, with this program, "we don't seek to cancel or approve any specific narrative, but rather to create a journey through the personal and national history of each side, through meaningful dialogue, respect, and understanding that each personal and national narrative holds a truth in it."[41] Its chief goal is to recognize and respect the stories of both sides without canceling or approving either side. The project offers insight into the different contexts of the stories and requires hermeneutic openness to listen to the other's stories to complete a picture. Participating in this dialogue allows the parties to listen to each other's con-texts and practice hermeneutic openness to understand the other side of the story, ultimately taking the vulnerable road to de-center their own experience.

This type of encounter, in which two people from different and often opposing sides of the conflict, can be translated into the different context of the positions within the dialogue contexts here in the West. Dialogue about the Land between Christians and Jews is not impossible. Recent developments both in the academic arena and in the ecclesial world, notably at the National Council of Churches, are reasons to be hopeful. The volume *Enabling Dialogue about the Land*, edited by Philip A. Cunningham, Ruth Langer, and Jesper Svartvik, is the outcome of years of conversations between Christians and Jews in various locations. It is a compilation of essays written by multiple voices, Jewish and Christian alike, and from diverse perspectives on the Land and provides further resources. To be sure, the editors never acknowledge their appropriation of comparative theological hermeneutics for their pursuit.

Nonetheless, the volume does provide a textual witness to a dialogue on the Land that honors the context of the contributing individuals.[42] Moreover, its achievements reveal a commitment to hermeneutic openness and humility.[43] How would the mosaic look like if, with such a commitment, we were able to mire the pieces of the various mosaic tiles each in their individual form and bring them together to see the larger mosaic that brings a new understanding of the contribution of every single tile within it?

NOTES

1. I use the terminology "Land" here because both in history and in the present people refer to it with so many different names, all of which carry theological meaning that also may be in dispute by others.
2. I refer here to a plural "Zionisms" because there is a variety of different ideologies, some only political, others religious. Some Zionist views are rooted in the

Jewish and others in the Christian tradition. These different views also carry different goals for their worldview. A recent introduction from David Novak gives an overview of Secular and religious Zionism in Judaism. Cf. Spector, *Evangelicals and Israel*, for the Christian side of things.
3. Svartvik, "Challenges and Guidelines," 243–44.
4. Langer, "Israel in Jewish Theologies," 43.
5. Langer, "Israel in Jewish Theologies," 44. Langer offers a perspective from a traditional Jewish lens. See also the statement "Reform Judaism and Zionism: A Centenary Platform" of the Central Conference of American Rabbis (1997), a body within the liberal reform movement.
6. Hertzberg, *The Zionist Idea*, 425.
7. Hertzberg, *The Zionist Idea*, 429.
8. Hertzberg, *The Zionist Idea*, 419.
9. Hertzberg, *The Zionist Idea*, 420–21.
10. Hertzberg, *The Zionist Idea*, 429.
11. Kessler, *An Introduction to Jewish-Christian Relations*, 24.
12. Spector, *Evangelicals and Israel*, 2. Spector's study gives insight into the various strands of Christian Zionism.
13. Spector, *Evangelicals and Israel*, 2.
14. Spector, *Evangelicals and Israel*, 24–29.
15. Haija, "The Armageddon Lobby," 82–84. Modern evangelical scholars like McDermott try to move away from this dispensationalist thought to a purely biblically rooted Zionism. cf. Gerald McDermott, *The New Christian Zionism*. However, evangelical institutions such as the International Christian Embassy in Jerusalem also clarify that most Christian Zionist would also agree that "Israel's reemergence on the world's scene, in fulfillment of God's promises to her, indicates that other events prophesied in the Bible will follow," referencing to the dispensationalist understanding Revelation. Cf. Hedding, "Biblical Christian Zionism 101."
16. Langer, "Israel in Jewish Theologies," 50.
17. To be sure, there are other important figures, most notably Moses Hess, Leo Pinsker, and Ber Borochov (who represents the Marxist side of the movement). In fact, Herzl borrowed several terms from Hess and Pinsker. In particular, Hess had been a promoter of Jewish nationalism and the regeneration of a Jewish nation. Cf. Dan Cohn-Sherbok, *Introduction to Zionism and Israel*, 3–6.
18. Hertzberg, *The Zionist Idea*, 204.
19. Hertzberg, *The Zionist Idea*, 205, 209.
20. Hertzberg, *The Zionist Idea*, 209.
21. Hertzberg, *The Zionist Idea*, 227.
22. Hertzberg, *The Zionist Idea*, 228.
23. Ateek, *A Palestinian Theology of Liberation*, 77–78.
24. Ateek, *A Palestinian Theology of Liberation*, 60–61.

25. Ateek, *A Palestinian Theology of Liberation*, 50.
26. Ateek, *A Palestinian Theology of Liberation*, 66. Other liberationist voices echo Ateek's positions. For instance, in an edited volume, Rosemary Radford Ruether and Marc H. Ellis compiled essays that argue for peace between Israelis and Palestinians on the grounds that the State of Israel accept the territories of Palestine. See Ellis and Ruether, *Beyond Occupation*.
27. Raheb, *I Am a Palestinian Christian*, 74.
28. Ellis, *Toward a Jewish Theology of Liberation*, 2, 93.
29. I am referring here to Gregerman's analysis of Ruether and Ateek in Gregerman, "Old Wine in New Bottles."
30. Declaration for a Just Peace Between Palestine and Israel, 33rd General Synod of the United Church of Christ (2021).
31. On Recognition That Israel's Laws, Policies, and Practices Constitute Apartheid Against the Palestinian People, 225th General Assembly of the Presbyterian Church (2022).
32. Clooney, *Theology After Vedānta*, 52–53.
33. Joslyn-Semiatkoski, *The More Torah the More Life*.
34. Cornille, *Meaning and Method in Comparative Theology*, 80.
35. Cornille, *Meaning and Method in Comparative Theology*, 116–48. Six possible ways of gaining new insight into one's own religious tradition: Intensification, rectification, reinterpretation, appropriation, recovery, and affirmation.
36. Moyaert, *Fragile Identities*, 198–99.
37. Moyaert, *Fragile Identities*, 200, 232.
38. Moyaert, *Fragile Identities*; Cornille, *Meaning and Method in Comparative Theology*, 115–16. Cornille highlights here that the ultimate goal of comparative theology is the enhancement of truth. Cf. also p. 24.
39. Tanner, *Theories of Culture*, 112–14.
40. Krell, "Decentering Judaism and Christianity," 482. Krell brings Kathryn Tanner into conversation with McClintock Fulkerson to argue for a theological approach of decentering.
41. Parents Circle Families Forum, "The Parallel Narrative Experience."
42. For instance, the volume contains the section "The Meaning of the Land" which comprises an article by a Jew, a Palestinian Christian, and a Muslim.
43. Cf. here, Cunningham's clarification that the dialogue did not seek to resolve the conflict in the preface of *Enabling Dialogue About the Land*.

REFERENCES

Ateek, Naim Stifan. *A Palestinian Theology of Liberation: The Bible, Justice, and the Palestine-Israel Conflict*. Maryknoll, NY: Orbis, 2017.

Clooney, Francis X. *Theology After Vedānta*. Albany: State University of New York Press, 1993.

Cohn-Sherbok, Dan. *Introduction to Zionism and Israel: From Ideology to History*. London: Continuum, 2012.

Cornille, Catherine. *Meaning and Method in Comparative Theology*. Hoboken, NJ: Wiley-Blackwell, 2020.

Cunningham, Philip A., Ruth Langer, and Jesper Svartvik, eds. *Enabling Dialogue About the Land: A Resource Book for Jews and Christians*. Mahwah, NJ: Paulist Press, 2020.

Declaration for a Just Peace Between Palestine and Israel. 33rd General Synod of the United Church of Christ (2021). https://www.globalministries.org/wp-content/uploads/2021/07/General-Synod-2021-Resolution-I-P.pdf.

Ellis, Marc H., *Toward a Jewish Theology of Liberation*. London: SCM Press, 2003.

Gregerman, Adam. "Old Wine in New Bottles." *Journal of Ecumenical Studies* 41, no. 3 (2004): 313–40.

Haija, Rammy M. "The Armageddon Lobby: Dispensationalist Christian Zionism and the Shaping of Us Policy Towards Israel-Palestine." *Holy Land Studies* 5, no. 1 (2006): 75–95. https://doi.org/10.3366/hls.2006.0006.

Hedding, Malcolm. "Biblical Christian Zionism 101." International Christian Embassy Jerusalem (ICEJ). Accessed January 29, 2023. https://www.icej.org/understand-israel/biblical-teachings/christian-zionism-101/.

Hertzberg, Arthur. *The Zionist Idea: A Historical Analysis and Reader*. Melrose Park, PA: Jewish Publication Society 1997.

Joslyn-Semiatkoski, Daniel. *The More Torah the More Life: A Christian Commentary on Mishnah Avot*. Leuven: Peeters Publishers, 2018.

Kessler, Edward. *An Introduction to Jewish-Christian Relations*. New York: Cambridge University Press, 2010.

Krell, Marc A. "Decentering Judaism and Christianity: Using Feminist Theory to Construct a Postmodern Jewish-Christian Theology." *Cross Currents* 50, no. 4 (2000): 474–87. https://www.jstor.org/stable/24460876.

Langer, Ruth. "Israel in Jewish Theologies: A Schematic Overview." In *Enabling Dialogue About the Land. A Resource Book for Jews and Christians*, edited by Ruth Langer Philip A. Cunningham, Jesper Svartvik, 43–62. Mahwah, NJ: Paulist Press, 2020.

McDermott, Gerald, R. *The New Christian Zionism: Fresh Perspectives on Israel and the Land*. Downers Grove, IL: IVP Books,

Moyaert, Marianne. *Fragile Identities: Toward a Theology of Interreligious Hospitality*. Amsterdam: Rodopi, 2011.

Novak, David. *Zionism and Judaism: A New Theory*. New York: Cambridge University Press, 2015.

On Recognition That Israel's Laws, Policies, and Practices Constitute Apartheid Against the Palestinian People. 225th General Assembly of the Presbyterian Church (2022). https://www.pc-biz.org/#/search/3000773.

Parents Circle Families Forum. "The Parallel Narrative Experience." Accessed January 29, 2023. https://www.theparentscircle.org/en/pcff-activities_eng/narrative-pne_eng/.

Raheb, Mitri. *I Am a Palestinian Christian*. Translated by Ruth C. L. Gritsch. Minneapolis: Augsburg Fortress, 1995.

"Reform Judaism & Zionism: A Centenary Platform." Central Conference of American Rabbis. Accessed January 29, 2023. https://www.ccarnet.org/rabbinic-voice/platforms/article-reform-judaism-zionism-centenary-platform/.

Ruether, Rosemary Radford and Marc H. Ellis, eds. *Beyond Occupation: American Jewish, Christian, and Palestinian Voices for Peace*. Boston: Beacon Press, 1990.

Spector, Stephen. *Evangelicals and Israel: The Story of American Christian Zionism*. Oxford: Oxford University Press, 2009.

Svartvik, Jesper. "Challenges and Guidelines for a Christian Theology of the Land." In *Enabling Dialogue about the Land: A Resource Book for Jews and Christians*, edited by Philip A. Cunningham, Ruth Langer, and Jesper Svartvik, 241–61. Mahwah, NJ: Paulist Press, 2020.

Tanner, Kathryn. *Theories of Culture: A New Agenda for Theology*. Minneapolis: Augsburg Fortress Press, 1997.

O'NEIL VAN HORN

THE PARADOXES OF PLACE

Cultivating Particularity and Planetarity Amid Climate Catastrophe

PRELUDE: HERE, THERE—WHERE?

Places are particular; yet, simultaneously, places are porous. That is, places suggest an expression of contextuality that need not imply impermeable boundedness; but, still, to be placed is to be precisely "here" and not "there." Naturally. But where does "here" end and "there" begin? Articulating such a question feels foolish, banal, even pedantic. But I am convinced that this question and its attendant paradoxes warrant critical philosophical and theological attention.

Intuitively, culturally, ecologically, we know well that "here" is not "there." But it's more than that, of course. For one, notions of "here" and "there" complicate ethics. To live well here may not constitute living well there. And so, too, the opposite is true. In a word, a place demands localized ethics, yet not necessarily at the expense of other bioregions. As Wendell Berry puts it, "The land is too various in its kinds, climates, conditions, declivities, aspects, and histories to conform to any *generalized understanding* or to prosper under *generalized treatment*."[1] At the edge of planetary catastrophe, generalized treatment of land will not suffice—nor will myopic treatment—given the complexities of geography, biodiversity, soil composition, not to mention climate. These are the lessons long stewarded by indigenous lifeways, agrarian philosophies, and contextual ethics alike. But the effect of location on ethics still does not answer the question that prefigures it, grounds it: Where exactly does a place begin and end? After all, how exactly does one conceive of the boundaries of bioregions, the edges of ecosystems? A tension emerges in the consideration of these inarticulable thresholds. Thus, the first paradox of place: places are located yet linked, contextual yet enmeshed.

But, there is also a further paradox at play here. Land (when read as ecologist Aldo Leopold would have it)[2] is not any one thing—not a concrete foundation, not even exactly *terra firma*, at least if we take seriously the teachings of contemporary soil science, process metaphysics, and systems ecology.[3] Places are not a set of objects; they are ever mattering networks of intertwined matters. The soily "substance" of land, while no doubt substantive, is hardly a "thing" at all: instead, that which grounds our existence, when considered through these process-oriented lenses, reveals itself to be a complex web of becomings, transitions, compositions, decompositions, movements, affects, energies. Places are, at best, unstably stable. Thus, the second paradox of place: places are simultaneously grounding and ungrounding.

What would it mean, then, to consider the rich theological potencies of these paradoxes? I intend to explore these matters by asking the following questions:

1) Might the traditions of apophatic theology, paradoxically, have something to say about the nigh unspeakable particularity and permeability of place? In other words, how might mystical negative theologies disclose—which is not exactly to say "make sense of"—the aporias that prefigure place? What might apophasis have to offer bioregionalism?
2) And, could the paradoxes of place illuminate novel modes of pluralistic, interreligious planetary politics in the Anthropocene? Might the revelations of place offer a vision for possibilities of cooperation across lines of critical differences—in which differences serve not as divisions but relations?

These questions will organize this work, each of which ground the subsections to follow. Should it not already be abundantly clear, this work is an experiment, seeking the edges of theopoetic discourse and traversing the borders of disciplines.

Ultimately, this article intends to offer a critical theoretical lens for land-based theologies; in other words, it explores that which conceptually grounds land-based theologies, asking what precisely is meant by "land" and "place." These reflections on place illuminate a way to understand the simultaneity of interconnection and radical difference, the concomitance of particularity and porosity, offering to comparative theology a conceptualization as to how places and their particularities/porosities disclose alternative ways to understand the particularities/porosities of religious traditions and identities. Sought here is a capacious and earthy pluralism in hopes that the disclosure of entangled diversity will cultivate creative efforts of environmental justice—honoring the unspeakable vitality of land without yielding to reductionistic, colonial, and capitalist logics of land as object, territory, background.

SPEAKING OF PLACES, UNSPEAKING OF PLACES: AN APOPHATIC BIOREGIONALISM

Before addressing the paradoxes revealed by notions of "place" and the potential value of negative theology in our treatments thereof, it is necessary to first explore the paradoxical, as such. Specifically, it is crucial to limn that which paradox solicits: how one responds, how one is undone, by paradox.

To speak of paradoxes in the affirmative can lead to the erasure of their truths—whether through supersession, whitewashing, or feigned transcendence. Unity (One) must not abolish discord (Many), but neither can the multiplicitous forsake the interconnections by which it is constituted. But the transgressive tensions of aporia need not stifle nor force stasis; they instead demand movement, discernment, meditation, creativity, even experimentation—at times constructive, at others deconstructive.

The reduction of paradoxes to tidy solutions destroys complexity in favor of homogeneity; and complexity, we know, is the precise element of health proffered by biodiversity;[4] to be theological about it, then, the collapse of paradox is often the precise consequence caused by the codified concretization of creeds and dictations of dogmas in institutionalized contexts.[5] The threat of concretization or reification always looms, keen to fashion divinity into sheer comprehensibility or, worse, an idol—as idols are often easy to wield in whatever ways one may please. By minimizing the aporetic, we minimize, if not devastate, mystery. Paradoxes have no ruler, no master. Yet in the desire for "closure"—whether ecclesial, intellectual, political, or beyond—the foreclosure of the wondrous openings of paradox suppresses the divine creativity they inspire.[6] And in some cases, namely in contexts of colonization and similar, this foreclosure is by design. The mark of the paradoxical is ongoingness, openness, unknowingness—pleats of sensible mystery that cannot entirely "make sense."

What can be said of that which shirks finality and resists closure? Isn't every utterance an arrest of the truth that one aims at—only ever partial, at best? If this is the case, then, perhaps, impossibly, could it yet be that *poiesis*, practiced here as theopoetics, is a "making" that's made possible through the very rift of apophasis that paradox inspires, indeed necessitates? Put differently, perhaps at the edges of language, where speech curls back in a gesture of becoming undone, it is through "unsaying" that we can speak most truthfully in response to, in the wake of, the paradoxical.

If places are porous and particular, grounding and ungrounding, how might one respond? To begin, one need not be stifled by these paradoxes, though one may well be undone by them. Anything other than an ongoing openness to these matters constitutes a suppression of their wisdoms. What precisely would it mean to be undone in this sense, and how might negative theology offer a way into these mysterious grounds?

What if we were simply to flip the conventional script on apophasis, as it were? By this I *don't* mean merely a negation of its terms so much as a reorientation of their direction: negative theology not for the sake of sheer transcendence so much as earthen immanence. I contend that through apophasis one will sense, if only darkly, the catalytic force of paradox, not engendering some skyward flight toward the transcendent but instead luring toward terrestrial tenderness and ecological affection—in ways that do not demand the calcification of particularities into superseding universalities.

The mystical awe into which one enters in the cloud of paradox, often only ever at the precipice of the communicable, unfolds new possibilities as they are simultaneously enfolded in the mists of this wonder. Following philosopher of religion Mary-Jane Rubenstein's proposal, what would it mean to "*stay with* the perilous wonder that resists final resolution, simple identity, and sure teleology?"[7] No such mastery of the wondrous is possible, lest one wish to foreclose these animacies into mere "things in themselves." The ecological promise of the apophatic, the wondrous, is hard to miss: Surely it is impossible to characterize bioregions with any sort of final resolution, simple identity, or sure teleology. The processual nature of nature abides by no such anthropocentric projections, despite how desperately many—neoliberal capitalists most egregiously—wish this were the case. Land is not a thing so much as an undulation of energies, an assemblage of affects, a rhizome of entangled matters.[8]

At the edges of speech, the borderlands of the articulable, words falter and declarations fall short. Apophatic theology, at its most constructive, offers "an incantation at the edge of uncertainty," in the words of theologian Catherine Keller.[9] Apophasis performs a necessary deconstructive function, fissuring transcendent universals pretending eternality; the act of unsaying, an actionless action,[10] acknowledges the ineptitude of speech to convey, much less capture, incomprehensibilities: of Earth, of divinity. Here, here in the face of sacred mystery, we are undone. Indeed, this undoing even exposes the porosities of that which prefigures "we."[11]

Central to many strands of negative theology is an interest in preventing the concretization of the divine into limited categories, essentialized concepts, or static substances. The negations that characterize this practice—ancient and contemporary—are neither for some sort of contrived, pious humility nor for mystification's sake alone. Far from it! It would seem that it is the unsaying, the deconstructing, the unmaking of notions of divinity that is precisely what keeps divinity *alive*—or, at the very least, as a live concept. As historian of mysticism Charles M. Stang contends, "The impulse behind perpetual negation, then, is a yearning for God that will accept no proxies—that is to say, no idols. Even our contemplations of the divine names must be sacrificed at the altar to the unknown God."[12] The refusal to capture, to arrest, to categorize that is embodied in unsaying can thus be extended to enlivening perspectives on places that preserve the vibrancies of lives, matters, and minerals therein. Thus, could it be that the fecundities of this practice can be grounded in the terrestrial, illuminating modes of relation that need not abandon bioregions altogether nor categorically render them as stagnant, self-same sets of substances or, worse, resources and territories?

Even if theological truth-claims do express divine realities faithfully, such longstanding transcendentals still materialize ever differentially. These contextual incarnations are thus spatio-temporally particular, geographically placed. Catalyzed here—that is, in the speechlessness of divine mystery—is none other than vibrant presence, incapable of codification or concretization, at least in any final sense. To be present is thus to attune oneself to place, to space. This attunement often appears to be less a "doing" and more an *undoing*, a relinquishing of one's self—especially the impulses influenced by capitalist narratives and colonial logics—to the here-now. Presence is thus a breaking open at the recognition of the simultaneity of interconnection and difference: I am I and yet I am a part of this ground—a multiplicity in the (un)making. Undoing as presence, presence as undoing, in short. Yet, becoming undone need not mean an ascendant ecstasy, removing one from earthen landscapes, but instead can assume a more muddied inflection, driving one to be rooted more deeply in the present—which is only ever spatio-temporally placed.

To this end, Dionysius the Areopagite (otherwise known as Pseudo-Dionysius), in his work, *Mystical Theology,* processes the forms of presence that precipitate at the fringes of the utterable. Dionysius shatters our imaginative ceilings precisely by heading in the opposite direction: "the more our words are confined to the ideas we are capable of forming; so that now as we plunge into that darkness which is beyond intellect, we shall find ourselves not simply running short of words but actually speechless and unknowing."[13] This unknowing plunge is not up and away, despite the popular connotations of mysticism as narrowly concerned with the supernatural; instead, the speechlessness intimated here constitutes a grounded intimacy. As Catherine Keller puts it, "The ascent is actually a plunge: the cloud circulates in an atmosphere that *undoes the very axis of up and down.*"[14] Of course, this collapse of transcendence and immanence has quite a history even in negative theological discourse.

Gregory of Nyssa's own contentions about the boundlessness of the divine lay the groundwork for eco-apophasis as an entanglement of an immanent transcendence, to play here with paradoxical language. For example, he writes, "For nothing is Divine that is conceived as being circumscribed, but it belongs to the Godhead to be in all places, and to pervade all things, and not to be limited by anything."[15] According to Gregory, God is limitless; if God were limited, as Keller explicates his position, "it would have to be by something greater than God."[16] Keller rightly asks, "And if God signifies the boundless, what boundary can lie between God and creation—between the infinite and the finite? The challenge to any Creator/Creation dualism follows immediately."[17] The ecological sensibilities here are obvious and abound. But Gregory's arguments resist sliding into some sort of flat pantheism; as Keller contends, ". . . while there is *no fixed boundary*, there is nonetheless a heightened *distinction* between creator and creation . . . The difference between the finite and the infinite appears as *infinite.* But *difference*—especially infinite difference—is not boundary, but *relation.*"[18] Difference need not imply divorce but is, as it happens, an inflection of relation. And if the earthen is shot through with the heavenly, so to speak (or, "on Earth as it is in Heaven," as they say), this revelation can merit no response other than, no reaction short of, utter undoing. It is here that a Gregorian mystical apophasis reveals its deconstructive capacities, folding and entangling the transcendent and immanent.

Key to the muddying of these mystical qualities is that of *eros*, of divine yearning. The function of *eros* in negative theologies combats not only the rather common accusations of Platonism (especially in reference to Dionysius) as necessitating an obsessive otherworldly myopia—thereby overlooking the embodied, the ecological, the eco-social—but, *further,* resists the assumption that apophasis inhibits any meaningful possibility of incarnational care.[19] As argued by Stang, in Dionysius's *The Divine Names* there appears to be a collapse of the distinction between *eros* and *agape*, with the Areopagite claiming, "it may be boldly said with truth that even the very Author of all things, by reason of overflowing Goodness, loves all, makes all, perfects all, sustains all, attracts all."[20] This yearning, evident here in Dionysius but also unfurling in the many subsequent erotically-charged mystical traditions, is deeply intertwined with apophatic commitments; the nature of divine love—for the divine, for one another, for Earth—often easily renders us speechless. And the inexpressible draws us *not* up-and-away but *instead* into deeper care: as Stang eloquently writes, "*Erōs* is the engine of apophasis, a yearning that stretches language to the point that it breaks, stretches the lover to the point that he splits."[21] To become undone in this way does not imply inactivity: speechlessness is indeed active, even in its silence. This undoing constitutes an opening for more intimate relations, for closer forms of knowing. Keller's expressiveness to this end cannot be adequately paraphrased:

> If we can embrace this insight—that the very desire that drives us beyond ourselves in earthly relations of attraction and of justice is that which drives us in and beyond speech, and that in this eros we are iterating and exercising the love that always already exceeds us—no paternalism of the distant and dysrelational transcendence can long remain erect upon the Neoplatonic peak.[22]

Unknowability and indeterminacy are not incompatible with divine compassion for the terrestrial; rather, *they are the very catalysts thereof!* Here, here in the luminous dark of apophasis, we find not a Neoplatonic concern for merely the heavenly but, to the contrary, an entanglement of immanence and transcendence, disclosing the infinitude implicit in the finite. Out of the flows of this unnameable undoing comes an *eros*-driven commitment to the *eco-*.

What then does apophatic theology explicitly offer to land-based theologies, to bioregional ethics? What is apophasis's relation to the paradoxes posed by land? What of negative theology's capacity to cultivate notions of place that are permeable and particular for the sake of their care?

For one, this practice discloses the deconstructive value of becoming undone as an embodiment of radical presence, fracturing any possible solution that purports universality. Places and their attendant paradoxes undermine, indeed decompose, any panacea: There is no panacea to the planetary, even as our particular planetary conditions intersect vitally, albeit differentially.

With any veritable commitment to contextuality and the apophatic, the two now intermingling, there is no finality, no final knowledge, and certainly no—G-d forbid—Final Solution. Bioregional ethics cannot, therefore, be predicated on closure so much as sustained presence—spatio-temporal, temporally-spatial. Bioregionalism, paradoxically, necessitates neither boundaries between the "here" and "there" nor even myopic fixations on the "here," even if not at the expense of "there." When bioregionalism is figured mistakenly in these ways, idols are fashioned of places: the land becomes a static object of manipulation (even if of wholesome and regenerative interaction) rather than the infinitely multiplex network of lively relations by which it is constituted. And yet, bioregionalism cannot forsake particularity, as bioregionalism without local foci would be a contradiction of terms. At the core of the paradoxes of place is the revelation of the *relation of difference*, the *nonseparability of difference*—which cannot be solved so much as encountered. That is, the speechlessness that accompanies an encounter with the unfathomable complexity of places—intersecting, overlapping, multiplying—intimates the revelation of the entanglement of each in each and all in all—all the while preserving the critical differences therein.[23] This is similar to the anonymous French anarchist collective The Invisible Committee's reflections on their suggested response to "fragmentation" (though in their case they are referring to the splintering of the social order at geopolitical levels): resistant to calls for undifferentiated unity—or, "generalized treatment," to recall Berry's language—one must instead embrace fragmentation as one's "starting point," as it were. In the parlance of this experimental article, it could be said that one must begin from a place of un/grounding: presence that draws one into relation and yet requires unknowing humility. The Invisible Committee writes:

> One rediscovers that opening oneself to the world doesn't mean opening oneself to the four corners of the planet, that the world is there where we are. Opening ourselves to the world is opening ourselves to its presence here and now. Each fragment carries its own possibility of perfection. If "the world" is to be saved this will be in each of its fragments. As for the totality, it can only be *managed*.[24]

Hence, this radical encounter with places, with the portion of the world to which we are present, can be considered neither complete subsumption (One) nor irreconcilable otherness (Many) so much as processual, plurisingular entanglements of compassion (Multiplicity). As The Invisible Committee suggests, this relational fragmentation can, unthinkably, "give rise to an intensification and pluralization of the bonds that constitute us. Then fragmentation doesn't signify separation but a shimmering of the world."[25] This shimmering could perhaps, to generously stretch the metaphor, be read as becoming undone by the multiplex nonseparabilities constituting our *oikos* as a form of radical terrestrial presence. To this end, Keller relatedly asks, ". . . what is the fold between our nonknowing and our nonseparability?"[26] If we mind our radical encounters with particular places and the care they inspire, that mindfulness "folds itself into its own plurisingularity, into a knowing-together that structures greater complexity and stabilizes wider cooperation. In other words, it stimulates responsive participation in entangled difference."[27] Or, ungrounding as a grounding principle for planetary politics.

What precisely would this mean, then, for an apophatic bioregionalism? It would imply that the porous and particular places that ground and suffuse us multiplicitously entangle themselves within and as our nonknowing, disclosing what Keller calls "the self-implication of relation" in which our apophatic minding of places "*knowingly folds multiplicity beyond knowing into a knowing together.*"[28] The function of apophasis is the revelation, then, that any knowing—including nonknowing—is only ever *knowing together.* The earthen inflections of the undoing proffered by radical encounters—placed, present—suggests the vast entanglements constituting the so-called epistemological, which always ought to carry the neglected prefix of *eco-*. Put simply, becoming undone in response to the nonseparability of difference prefigured by places carves space for unfolding earthen epistemologies aimed at environmental justice. This ungrounding, in a word, opens us to the genius of place.[29]

An unknowing bioregionalism breaks open foreclosures, ungrounding our certainties without eliding the need for resolute commitments to justice-seeking. This way-making presence would lead to powerful forms of relation that are not marked by power as "power over" so much as an honoring of the indeterminacy and unknowability of the complexities of our *oikos*. This does not imply the refusal to act, much less to restore or salvage or remediate, but it does demand the processual curling back, reassessment, reattunement in response to the ongoing relations of becoming by which places are prefigured. An apophatic bioregional ethic catalyzes—not suppresses—resolute decisions for the sake of wholesomeness. Keller succinctly conveys this very concern: "The point would not be then to cordon off the unknowable—for by definition we cannot know where it begins, since we don't *know* it—but to *mind* its impinging indeterminacies. The opening into an uncertainty at the heart of things need not then dishearten decision."[30] Uncertainty heartens, provoking adaptation to flux. It is thus simultaneously a deeply ecological and theological revelation revealed by the paradoxes of place: the unthinkable entanglement of difference.

ORGANIZING IN PLACE: INTERRELIGIOUS PLANETARY POLITICS

If finding presence amid the paradoxes of place discloses an undoing in service of the earthen—without forsaking the infinitude with which the finite is shot through—might this offer a mode of interreligious engagement resistant to the injustices both causing and caused by climate change? Further, could the revelations of land, articulable tersely as "the entanglement of difference," reveal a notion of pluralism sufficient to withstand the trials of the Anthropocene? And might the paradoxes of land reveal themselves as phenomena that might assist in reimagining our conceptualizations of religious traditions and identities—especially the interconnections between and intra-actions therein?

What are, as Catherine Keller and philosophical theologian Roland Faber put it, the "connective preconditions" grounding both expressions of religiosity and climate justice-seeking coalitions?[31] Given the complex and porous notions of what exactly constitutes a "religion," let alone what "separates" it from other traditions (not to mention from other facets of life), the aim here is not to concoct the "Least Common Denominator" underlying various religious expressions; such a practice reifies the flattening functions of the well-intended but often harm-producing notion of "common ground," erasing—or, if nothing else, whitewashing—the critical and enlivening differences between, within, among. To this end, comparative theologian John Thatamanil incisively argues, "the notion of a singular religious identity, in circular fashion, is generated by and in turn generates the idea that religions are neatly separated by clearly demarcated and impermeable borders."[32] Sought here is thus not the overlording and colonizing Oneness, inventing universals where there are none, nor the erection of "impermeable borders," as warned by Thatamanil; instead, I ask very simply, what is that which *grounds* pluralistic collectives?

If the previous section has offered anything, it is that land—indeed, the *earth-ground*—does not constitute a smoothing foundationalism, as the paradoxes of place decompose any such attempt to proffer panaceas. That which grounds us, as we have seen, suggests the nonseparability of difference, the vision of communal lures that enter into relation with the differential characteristics of their place. Wendell Berry has argued this point for decades now: "A culture capable of preserving land and people can be made only within a relatively stable and enduring relationship between a local people and its place. Community cultures made in this way would *necessarily differ*, and sometimes radically so, from one place to another, *because places differ*. This is the true and necessary pluralism."[33] This, of course, has been the heart of indigenous lifeways and traditional environmental knowledge all along.

The particularities, which is also to say the paradoxes, of places reveal pluralism as always already existing—most expressly at the terrestrial level. Pluralism need not—indeed must not—be read here as harmonious union, the romanticization of unity at the expense of recognizing particularities that remain in tension. Still, that the planetary is neither separable nor smooth, unrelated nor homogenous, hints at an eco-mimetic observation: our grounding condition as heterogeneously yet nonseparably entangled.

The goal here, hence, is not the *creation* of pluralism so much as a (re)attunement thereto. Given the particularities of places—the critical differences entangled in and as limitless locales—any legitimately robust resistance to climate injustice could only be marked by a commitment to *multiplicity*.

With multiplicity comes the deconstruction and deterritorialization of any abstract universal in favor of context-specific, place-based, bioregional concerns—ever in process, wherein the processual obliges nonknowing. And wouldn't this multiplicitous assemblage simply foreground the obvious eco-ethical syncretisms that have always been the case: place and praxis concomitantly composing and decomposing one another? By taking on the revelations of place—as generated by the paradoxes thereof—interreligious climate resistance may yet promise deeper resonances and potent amplifications through a nonknowing that is not a wholesale renunciation of truth or facts or even doctrine or creed but is, rather, a *knowing together*. And "knowing together," as it happens, is but a relational reading of *con-sciousness*. And yet, like the ongoingness that defines the sort of presence that allows one to attune to the intricacies, indeed intimacies, of place, this form of coalitional praxis does not strip communities of their particularities in service of some undifferentiated, homogenous One, effacing all in service of a bland, often white, foundationalist "common ground;" rather, it is this nonknowing that engenders the meaningful relations among critical differences, provoking a place-based pluralism.

The pluralities of religions and the pluralities of place thus mirror one another: porous yet particular, grounding and ungrounding. The intention, then, of any land-based theology (especially of the comparative sort) must not be to seek multiplicity "across" religious traditions, fallaciously mistaking religions as their abstractions—neatly separable and perfectly discrete—instead of as their complex earthen manifestations,[34] but rather multiplicity as the rhizomatic interdependence that renders boundaries and border-walls viscous and fuzzy.[35] Put differently, it's the admission that multiplicity complicates every such tradition—not merely implying that traditions are "complex" but, further, that traditions are a *complicatio*—enfolding and unfolding the differences that ground them. Or, as Keller and Faber suggest, any robust and responsible pluralism must neither assemble "a mere many" separate traditions—now in some jumbled heap—nor fall prey to the colonial logics of a curatorial, often fetishizing, "collection" of appropriated traditions; instead, they propose a polydoxical pluralism, which "displays the folds of a wisdom [they] find only in multi*pli*city: the *pli,* which makes the difference connective and opens the connections into difference."[36] Differences as connective, particularities as relations—these are the paradoxical wisdoms that any theology of, on, and for land must assume for the sake of more rigorously pluralistic communions. Hence, these places, these traditions, it seems, are not exactly separable, even as their differences constitute the very possibility of planetary interconnection.

It seems then, I would contend, that any efforts of the comparative and/or pluralistic sort—whether academic, activist, or beyond—would behoove from attention to the terrestrial and theological paradoxes that solicit our undoings, as this does not draw us inward into solipsism but instead provokes unanticipable possibilities for fecund communions.

If presence is grounded in and by nonknowing—for presence is contingent upon mindful listening (for why would one listen if one already *Knows?*)—it is always already stitched into the relational folds of its environs. A critically diverse coalition that honors this would neither result in a self-interested apathy nor an isolated encampment so much as a commitment to land refusing to capitulate to colonial logics of territorialization. The ungrounding function of land thus suggests that land can neither be relinquished as unimportant—whether externalized as disposable or as necessary "collateral damage" of toxic capitalist industry—nor rendered as "object," even "nation."

POSTLUDE: UNKNOWING TOGETHER— DIVERSELY, DIFFERENTIALLY

Critical questions remain, offered here as an invitation for future work (and as a trajectorial point of connection to the other articles in this journal). And perhaps it is fitting, anyway, for the terminus of this experimental article to reverberate forth not with concrete claims of the "Knowledge" produced here but instead through invitational questions—queries that might lure both author and reader into forms of knowing together that are only possible when undone in unknowing: For those who reside on stolen land, colonized soils, settled contexts—of which I am included as a complicit and privileged beneficiary—there is no evading the legacies of theft, coercion, enslavement, genocide. Might the terrestrial aporias limned here unveil modes for interrelation across difference—of ecology, of religion—that recognize these toxic legacies yet do not foreclose novel avenues for meaningful communions grounded in principles of justice, equity, repair, wholesomeness? Might the aporetic serve a critical function in encountering—and perhaps, eventually, meaningfully repairing—the unthinkable evils committed by colonial regimes and capitalist endeavors by neither attempting to "make sense" of them (for any attempt to make meaning of these atrocities often implicitly justifies them) but also not neglecting their continued influence on our impure present?[37] If so, what novel approaches to matters of sovereignty and reparations would emerge? Moved by the relation of difference (i.e. the revelations of land), what sociopolitical promises persist for rendering land as neither "object" nor "nation" but as that which grounds our differential becomings? Only at the unspeakable edges of imagination, I think, might we envisage lifeways in service of these vital uncertainties.

NOTES

1. Berry, *The Unsettling of America*, 35; emphasis mine.
2. As Aldo Leopold, in his seminal essay, "The Land Ethic," describes, "Land, then, is not merely soil; it is a fountain of energy flowing through a circuit of soils, plants, and animals. Food chains are the living channels which conduct energy upward; death and decay return it to the soil." Leopold, *A Sand County Almanac*, 253.
3. See, for example, Lehmann and Kleber, "The Contentious Nature of Soil Organic Matter;" Schmidt, et. al., "Persistence of Soil Organic Matter as an Ecosystem Property;" Baskin, *Under Ground*; Barad, *Meeting the Universe Halfway*; Bennett, *Vibrant Matter*; Bruno Latour, *Reassembling the Social*.
4. See, for example, Shiva, *Biopiracy*, esp. 65–86.
5. See Tillich, *Dynamics of Faith*, 25–34. See also Keller, *On the Mystery*, 9–25.
6. See Rubenstein, *Strange Wonder*, esp. 1–24.
7. Rubenstein, *Strange Wonder*, 23.
8. While merely theorizing these conceptual possibilities and their eco-ethical outflows does little, if anything at all, to stop those who master, mine, and marshal the more-than-human, it does indeed offer a conceptual intervention for those with ears to hear—and, hopefully, for the sake of bolstering a counter-power to the Powers that Be.
9. Keller, *Face of the Deep*, xviii.
10. That is, it is reminiscent of the Taoist notion of *wu-wei*. See, for example, Slingerland, *Effortless Action*; Alan Fox, "Reflex and Reflectivity: *Wuwei* in the *Zhuangzi*."
11. Queer theorist Judith Butler's meditations on the undoing that occurs in the wake of grief discloses a resonant relational ontology: "It is not as if an 'I' exists independently over here and then simply loses a 'you' over there, especially if the attachment to 'you' is part of what composes who I am. . . . Who 'am' I, without you? When we lose some of these ties by which we are constituted, we do not know who we are or what to do." Butler, *Precarious Life*, 22.
12. Stang, *Apophasis and Pseudonymity in Dionysius the Areopagite*, 169.
13. Pseudo-Dionysius, *Mystical Theology*, 139.
14. Keller, *Cloud of the Impossible*, 73.
15. Stang, "Negative Theology from Gregory of Nyssa to Dionysius the Areopagite," 169.
16. Keller, *Cloud of the Impossible*, 62. See Gregory of Nyssa, *The Life of Moses*, 115–16: "He learns from what was said that the Divine is by its very nature infinite, enclosed by no boundary. If the Divine is perceived as though bounded by something, one must by all means consider along with that boundary what is beyond it. For certainly that which is bounded leaves off at some point, as air provides the boundary for all that flies and water for all that live in it. Therefore, fish are surrounded on every side by water, and birds by air. The limits of the boundaries which circumscribe the birds or the fish are obvious:

The water is the limit to what swims and the air to what flies. In the same way, God, if he is conceived as bounded, would necessarily be surrounded by something different in nature. It is only logical that what encompasses is much larger than what is contained."

17. Keller, *Cloud of the Impossible*, 62.
18. Keller, *Cloud of the Impossible*, 62–63.
19. For a more expansive take on Dionysius, see Keller, *Cloud of the Impossible*, 67–78.
20. Stang, *Apophasis and Pseudonymity in Dionysius the Areopagite*, 169.
21. Stang, *Apophasis and Pseudonymity in Dionysius the Areopagite*, 169–70.
22. Keller, *Cloud of the Impossible*, 76.
23. The invocation of "each in each" and "all in all" is a riff on both Nicholas of Cusa as well as Alfred North Whitehead: see Nicholas of Cusa, *De Docta Ignorantia*, 140; Alfred N. Whitehead, *Process and Reality*, 50.
24. The Invisible Committee, *Now*, 23.
25. The Invisible Committee, *Now*, 43.
26. Keller, *Cloud of the Impossible*, 286.
27. Keller, *Cloud of the Impossible*, 287.
28. Keller, *Cloud of the Impossible*, 287.
29. See Jackson, *Consulting the Genius of the Place*.
30. Keller, *Cloud of the Impossible*, 231.
31. Faber and Keller, "A Taste for Multiplicity: The Skillful Means of Religious Pluralism," 184.
32. Thatamanil, "Comparative Theology After 'Religion,'" 243. For more on the hegemonic pitfalls of some expressions of so-called "comparative theology," see Tiemeier, "Comparative Theology as a Theology of Liberation."
33. Berry, *The Art of the Commonplace,* 180; emphasis mine.
34. This sort of thinking would constitute what process philosopher Alfred N. Whitehead terms the "Fallacy of Misplaced Concreteness." Whitehead explains, "There is an error; but it is merely the accidental error of mistaking the abstract for the concrete." He then expands, " . . . if we desired to obtain a more fundamental expression of the concrete character of natural fact, the element in this scheme which we should first criticise is the concept of simple location . . . among the primary elements of nature as apprehended in our immediate experience, there is no element whatever which possesses this character of *simple location* . . . I hold that by a process of constructive abstraction we can arrive at abstractions which are the simply located bits of material, and at other abstractions which are the minds included in the scientific scheme. Accordingly, the real error is an example of what I have termed: The Fallacy of Misplaced Concreteness." Put differently, this fallacy occurs when one mistakes an abstraction for material reality. Whitehead, *Science and the Modern World*, 52, 58.
35. Cf. Morton, *Dark Ecology*, 71–77.

36. Faber and Keller, 186; see also, Deleuze, *The Fold*.
37. See Shotwell, *Against Purity*.

REFERENCES

Barad, Karen. *Meeting the Universe Halfway: Quantum Physics and the Entanglement of Matter and Meaning*. Durham, NC: Duke University Press, 2007.

Baskin, Yvonne. *Under Ground: How Creatures of Mud and Dirt Shape Our World*. Washington, DC: Island Press, 2005.

Bennett, Jane. *Vibrant Matter: A Political Ecology of Things*. Durham, NC: Duke University Press, 2010.

Berry, Wendell. *The Art of the Commonplace: The Agrarian Essays of Wendell Berry*. Edited by Norman Wirzba. Berkeley, CA: Counterpoint, 2002.

———. *The Unsettling of America: Culture and Agriculture*. Berkeley, CA: Counterpoint, 2015.

Butler, Judith. *Precarious Life: The Powers of Mourning and Violence*. London: Verso, 2004.

Deleuze, Gilles. *The Fold: Leibniz and the Baroque*. Translated by Tom Conley. Minneapolis: University of Minnesota Press, 1993.

Faber, Roland and Catherine Keller. "A Taste for Multiplicity: The Skillful Means of Religious Pluralism." In *Religions in the Making: Whitehead and the Wisdom Traditions of the World*, edited by John B. Cobb, Jr., 180–207. Eugene, OR: Wipf and Stock, 2012.

Fox, Alan. "Reflex and Reflectivity: *Wuwei* in the *Zhuangzi*." *Asian Philosophy* 6, no. 1 (1996): 59–72. https://doi.org/10.1080/09552369608575428.

Gregory of Nyssa, *The Life of Moses*. New York: Paulist Press, 1978.

The Invisible Committee. *Now*. Translated by Robert Hurley. South Pasadena, CA: Semiotext(e), 2017.

Jackson, Wes. *Consulting the Genius of the Place: An Ecological Approach to a New Agriculture*. Berkeley, CA: Counterpoint, 2010.

Keller, Catherine. *Cloud of the Impossible: Negative Theology and Planetary Entanglement*. New York: Columbia University Press, 2015.

———. *Face of the Deep: A Theology of Becoming*. New York: Routledge, 2003.

———. *On the Mystery: Discerning Divinity in Process*. Minneapolis: Fortress Press, 2008.

Latour, Bruno. *Reassembling The Social: An Introduction to Actor-Network-Theory*. Oxford: Oxford University Press, 2005.

Lehmann, Johannes and Markus Kleber. "The Contentious Nature of Soil Organic Matter." *Nature* 528 (2015): 60–68. https://doi.org/10.1038/nature16069.

Leopold, Aldo. *A Sand County Almanac: And Sketches Here and There*. Oxford: Oxford University Press, 1966.

Morton, Timothy. *Dark Ecology: For a Logic of Future Coexistence*. New York: Columbia University Press, 2016.

Nicholas of Cusa. *De Docta Ignorantia.* In *Nicholas of Cusa: Selected Spiritual Writings*, translated by H. Lawrence Bond, 85–206. New York: Paulist Press, 1997.

Pseudo-Dionysius. *Mystical Theology.* In *Pseudo-Dionysius: The Complete Works*, translated by Colm Luibheid, 133–42. New York: Paulist Press, 1987.

Rubenstein, Mary-Jane. *Strange Wonder: The Closure of Metaphysics and the Opening of Awe.* New York: Columbia University Press, 2008.

Schmidt, Michael W., et. al. "Persistence of Soil Organic Matter as an Ecosystem Property." *Nature* 478 (2011): 49–56. https://doi.org/10.1038/nature10386.

Shiva, Vandana. *Biopiracy: The Plunder of Nature and Knowledge.* Berkeley, CA: North Atlantic Books, 1999.

Shotwell, Alexis. *Against Purity: Living Ethically in Compromised Times.* Minneapolis: University of Minnesota Press, 2016.

Slingerland, Edward G. *Effortless Action: Wu-wei as Conceptual Metaphor and Spiritual Ideal in Early China.* New York: Oxford University Press, 2003.

Stang, Charles M. *Apophasis and Pseudonymity in Dionysius the Areopagite: 'No Longer I.'* Oxford: Oxford University Press, 2012.

———. "Negative Theology from Gregory of Nyssa to Dionysius the Areopagite." In *The Wiley-Blackwell Companion to Christian Mysticism,* edited by Julia A. Lamm, 161–76. Malden: Blackwell, 2013.

Thatamanil, John J. "Comparative Theology After 'Religion.'" In *Planetary Loves: Spivak, Postcoloniality, and Theology*, edited by Mayra Rivera and Stephen D. Moore, 238–57. New York: Fordham University Press, 2011.

Tiemeier, Tracy Sayuki. "Comparative Theology as a Theology of Liberation." In *The New Comparative Theology: Thinking Interreligiously in the 21st Century*, edited by Francis X. Clooney, 129–49. New York: T&T Clark, 2010.

Tillich, Paul. *Dynamics of Faith.* New York: Harper Collins, 1957.

Whitehead, Alfred N. *Process and Reality: An Essay in Cosmology*. Corrected edition, edited by David Ray Griffin and Donald Sherburne. New York: Free Press, 1978.

———. *Science and the Modern World.* New York: Free Press, 1925.

HESRON H. SIHOMBING

THE BATAK-CHRISTIAN THEOLOGY OF LAND
Towards a Postcolonial Comparative Theology

COMPARATIVE THEOLOGY AND POSTCOLONIALITY
Comparative theology emerged as an epistemological strategy that honored the particularity of different faith traditions while also facilitating collaboration. It promotes interfaith dialogue, with enriching processes grounded in theological interactions between different religious traditions. While its focus supports shared learning through comparison of various religious/theological ideas, some scholars have expressed dissatisfaction with its epistemology, method, and purpose, especially with regard to the postcolonial context, methods, and theories.

Paul Hedges, a scholar in interreligious studies, for example, has poignantly argued that comparative theology has much invested in categorically Western frameworks. Hedges suggests that to elevate the potential of comparative theology, we must decolonize the method by moving beyond the dominant Western frameworks.[1] One way to do this is to pay attention to how the definition of religion is constructed based on a Protestant characterization that defines religion by its dogmatic predisposition. Such an understanding of religion oversimplifies the complex reality of religion in order to focus on belief, faith, and dogmatic teaching. The primacy of belief over practice in this kind of epistemological structure would distort religion, as it fails to recognize the importance of practices in defining what religion means. As much as a religion might be believed, religion is also lived and observed through different practices, festivals, events, and rituals. In fact, in some faith traditions, indigenous religions included, the existence of a well-structured faith confession may be optional, as religious obedience and observance are determined more significantly by the performance of specific rituals and mundane, daily practices.

Hedges further elaborates that comparative theology was birthed from a Western location and featured as a Christian (mainly Catholic) project.

Hedges notes that comparative theology has characteristically portrayed religions within the World Religions Paradigm (WRP), in which religion is principally considered as "textual, elite, cognitive, and defined by discrete and isolated traditions."[2] Tomoko Masuzawa, a Japanese-American scholar of comparative literature and history, has criticized WRP as an academic discipline and system of classification that seeks to maintain "a racialized notion of ethnic difference" by constructing differences that separate the West from the rest of the world under controllable signifiers and categorization.[3] In this system, the West is celebrated as progressive, and the East is configured as venerable; as Masuzawa puts it, "the East preserves history; the West creates history."[4] Within this system, the category of historical progress is determined by textuality, writing, literateness, and cognition. Hence, religions that do not conform to these features may have to adjust or assimilate themselves to comparative theology projects or risk having no unique place in this field.

WRP has further created the distinction between so-called great religions and little traditions. The little traditions are those faith traditions that do not fit the East-West distinction. In the past, they were often called "primitive religions," and such indigenous religions could be absorbed into the system but not taken seriously. That is probably why comparative theology has invested much in "World Religions" or the so-called "Big Five" religions,[5] leading to minimal attention being given to indigenous religions within comparative theology as a field of study. Since comparative theology focuses on doctrinal and theological comparison between well-constructed religions that fit Western standards, some indigenous religions that deviate from that mold have often been excluded from the development of comparative theology. In line with this, Tracy Tiemeier, a comparative theologian of Asian religions, has criticized the Western and predominantly Christian hegemonic tendency in comparative theology, and has advocated for more works to consider non-Christian and underrepresented traditions.[6]

Another notable dissatisfaction with conventional comparative theology lies in its neglect of the social matrix of power that influences the process of theological construction. Some works compare the theological particularities of two religions without regard for the practitioners' social context and lived experience, nor for the tension and shifts that occur over a tradition's history.[7] Projects in comparative theology often seem to focus overtly on the notion of neutrality rather than subjectivity, despite attempts to respect particularities. Comparative theology that truly favors deep particularities should consider both living traditions and textual sources. When traditions, as practiced and lived by practitioners within social matrices, are taken more seriously, particularities and subjectivity emerge as essential features. Religious texts may read the same, but how they are understood, contextualized, ritualized, and practiced may differ across various social locations. Consequently, decolonizing comparative theology must involve observing local religious phenomena and the analysis of social matrices of power beyond traditional textual exegesis. For this reason, this essay follows Talal Asad's configuration of religion as a historical construct shaped by disciplinary power. Religion cannot be universally defined because it is historically specific.[8]

Another important critique of comparative theology is its emphasis on frameworks of conceptual construction over matrices of historical power. Michel Foucault has called our attention to the importance of analyzing power relations. He emphasizes the need to consider the existence of power relations within knowledge production. "Power produces knowledge," and both imply one another. Power relations can exist through the construction of knowledge, while knowledge simultaneously also constitutes power relations.[9] Hence, the process of constructing and comparing various theological notions cannot abandon the dynamics of power-knowledge relations. In the same tone as Foucault, what post/decoloniality can bring to comparative theology is recognition of the significance of not only these power-knowledge relations but also of social location in the postcolonial context and the history of colonization as vital in understanding power-knowledge dynamics.[10] Power-knowledge relations in the postcolonial context manifest themselves in terms of knowledge production (epistemology) in order to create what Foucault calls "docility-utility."[11] Colonial power constructs, forms, and shapes knowledge to impose submission on its colonized subjects so that they can be utilized to maintain power and control for profit. For this reason, epistemology (knowledge production) cannot be separated from colonial domination and utility. Anibal Quijano coined the term "coloniality of power" to express the colonial formation of knowledge and social order in the colonized world that intersects with Eurocentrism and capitalism.[12] Expanding on Quijano's coloniality of power, Walter Mignolo and Catherine Walsh elaborate on "coloniality," the logic of colonial epistemology that creates the illusion of modernity among colonized subjects and nature. The structures of this illusion are what Mignolo and Walsh call "the colonial matrix of power."[13]

Paying attention to the coloniality of power will help comparative theology to address the postcolonial context. Comparing theologies in light of postcoloniality/decoloniality may contribute to investigating what Edward Said calls "the configurations of power":[14] the force and relationship of power between faith traditions, theologies, races, cultures, and regions. Examining forces of power shapes comparative theology in ways that interact with the lived experience of the colonized people to whom one theological idea is appealing and relevant. Comparative theology in the postcolonial context investigates the history of domination and colonization and gives space to how the colonized subjects' subjectivity and relationship to the topic under investigation may have changed throughout time because of the knowledge-power force (colonial matrix of power). Accordingly, no theological idea can be treated as if it exists in a vacuum—as if its historical construction has no bearing on its ramifications in the present and how it is manifested in practice is irrelevant. A genuine theology is always a lived theology as much as it is a spatialized theology that seeks understanding as it is practiced within the context of a particular space. A clear distinction and separation between theology as theory and theology as praxis does not serve comparative theology's original purpose of fostering interfaith learning.

Understanding the forces behind knowledge production in the postcolonial context suggests may require comparative theology to reexamine distinct, rigid boundaries drawn between faith traditions. This outlook recognizes that religions in the postcolonial world diverge from the categories the West has traditionally used. In this new context, flux, flow, and change may be the defining features of a religion, as people embrace elements of an imported religion while still adhering to and practicing their own indigenous religion(s). The continuous exchanges between imported religions and indigenous religions should not be seen as unwarranted challenge to comparative theology but as an opportunity to comprehend comparative theology anew. As such, comparative theology's strength may not be found in its respect for the particularities of traditions as separate, distinct essences but in the liberative potential of examining traditions as entangled and interrelated. A postcolonial comparative theology must—in the words of Jamaican-British cultural theorist Stuart Hall—"go beyond" the colonial paradigm. It opposes and critiques colonial paradigms and practices both as "a system of rule, of power, and exploitation" and a "system of knowledge and representation."[15] It seeks to identify the different forms of oppression and domination that one religious tradition may exert over another, but it also seeks to liberate both the oppressed and the oppressor from the paradigm of coloniality. Paul S. Chung, a Korean-born public theologian, contends that comparative theology should be "a way of encouraging each religious community to heed the source of solidarity and emancipation in its own tradition and context."[16] Tiemeier calls this epistemological effort "comparative theology of liberation."[17]

THE THEOLOGY OF THE LAND: AN INSIGHT FROM BATAK WISDOM

This section focuses on analyzing a local context in order to understand the global. Considering Kim Knott's spatial analysis of religion, specifying the social context is methodologically vital when discussing religious spatiality. Knott argues that to understand religion globally, we need to learn about it locally and vice versa.[18] More importantly, Knott's argument speaks well to how we should consider religion as transmitting through space. Religion must "exist and express itself in and through space, and must play its part in the constitution of spaces."[19] Because religion is inherently social, the construction of space in a religious setting or theological conviction must also consider that a religious space is also a social space imbued with power. The discussion of this essay considers the theology of the land in the Batak community of Indonesia from the lens of Knott's social space. We will see later that the Batak theology of the land, when compared with a colonial/Christian theology of the land, reveals the transmission of religion within Batakland as the critical point in understanding social space.

In relation to comparative theology, the argument made here is that comparative theology accordingly needs to consider a particular context and expression of texts/belief as indispensable to understanding a postcolonial comparative theology. Comparing an indigenous religion with an imported religion in a particular social setting would mean less theological construction than theological loss, modification, and hybridity. Comparison allows for an honest reflection on what has been lost from indigenous traditions, recognizes how certain theological conceptions have been modified and shaped through history, and investigates how certain theologies form hybrid constructs and identities as two distinctive worldviews encounter each other within an imbalanced matrix of power.

One way—but not the only way—to conduct postcolonial comparative theology is to compare two distinct theological ideas as living traditions within one community. We investigate how one community has lived these two different theologies simultaneously throughout history. However, comparative theology has always promoted faithfulness to one's particular faith tradition (home tradition) when venturing into other traditions to learn fresh theological insights. Francis X. Clooney, in seeking to construct a discrete definition of comparative theology, contends that it is "a reflective and contemplative endeavor by which we see the other in light of our own, and our own in the light of the other."[20] Thus, the distinction between home tradition and visited tradition—us and the other—remains intact and rigid. Postcolonial comparative theology offers a different approach to understanding multiple traditions, not as rigid but as hybrid traditions.[21] A particular postcolonial community may find faithfulness to just one tradition an impossible task when they have embraced multiple traditions simultaneously. Although comparative work between two traditions can still be done, learning must proceed from the fluid movement of history and space to understanding the movement of theological ideas, not the other way around. We look at how history and space influence and inform compared theologies and examine them without assuming that there is a tradition of departure nor a tradition of venture.

Batak is an Indonesian ethnic group that originates from Sumatra Island. It comprises six branches—the Toba, the Karo, the Simalungun, the Pak Pak, the Mandailing, and the Angkola—who speak distinct languages with some shared commonalities. At present, the majority of Batak people, especially the Batak Toba, are Christians, the largest group of whom embrace Lutheranism. I focus here on the Batak Toba people whose indigenous practices centered around worshiping the High God *Mulajadi Nabolon*.[22] Unless otherwise indicated, any following uses of "Batak" will refer to the Batak Toba. Anicetus B. Sinaga, a Batak-Christian theologian, has indicated that *Mulajadi Nabolon* is the eternal, everlasting, without beginning, and almighty Creator.[23] Batak people also call Mulajadi Nabolon *ompu*, which literally means "grandparent" but refers more deeply to entities who own superior power, dignity, and holiness.[24] The creation process includes the creation of the three Gods (*Batara Guru*, the creator; *Soripada*, the arranger; and *Mangala Bulan*, the judge) that reflect the personified works of Mulajadi Nabolon. There are also *Debata Asiasi*, the god of mercy; *Debata Idup*, the god of fertility; *Boru Saniang Naga*, the goddess of water; and other gods, goddesses, and spirits (including ancestral ones) who inhabit mountains, rivers, fields, forests, and other places.[25]

Batak people already had their distinct indigenous worldview encompassing their whole life. Religion is better understood as a historically constructed worldview that includes religion, culture, language, economy, and politics, all united in one single unit called *adat* (custom). It is imperative to remember that the spread of Christianity in Indonesia came with European colonization and modernization, which represent the forces of power mentioned above. Hence, when Rhenish missionaries began working in Batakland in the nineteenth century, they encountered people of a unique civilization strange to the Europeans. The direct encounter between Batak *adat* and the Rhenish missionaries, Dutch colonizers, and European modernity resulted in real struggles on the ground about how the Christian message ought to be planted in Batak culture. The struggles imply a sense of acceptance with a condition: rejection of the Batak culture considered opposed to the pietist-spirited doctrines of European Christianity, including, for this essay, the theology of the land.

Bungaran Simanjuntak has explored some Bataknese ideas about land. Bungaran identifies several kinds of land according to their functions in Batak culture: *tano tarulang* (empty/untouched land), *tano na niulang* (intentionally abandoned land), *harangan/tombak* (forest), *hauma* (rice field), *pargadongan* (non-rice field), *tano parhutaan* (residential land/village), *jalangan/jampalan* (farming areas with pasture), and *parmualan* (wetland for the water source). Batak land is centered on its use as a village (*huta*) located in *tano parhutaan*, residential land, a local area organized around ten to twenty-five houses, yards, streets, farms, springs/water source (*mual*), village borders, barns, cemetery, carpentry area, ritual/ceremony place, and others. *Huta* was the center of the Batak people's activities in relation to their land and community. One *huta* was occupied by one group of people from one family name and one ancestry. If the main village was already crowded, members could start a new village in a nearby location.[26] While *huta* is one among the various categorizations of land, it functionally signifies the interrelatedness of humans, God, and nature.

What is important to note is that land, according to the Batak people, does not primarily signify wealth or property. The land was defined through relationships, and vice versa; the relationships among people were expressed through the land. Land represents one's social connection to family and community. It brings together relationships and connections with the larger family and society. Achim Sibeth puts it correctly that the Batak people's social position is determined by how they relate socially with the other inhabitants of the village within the bounds of reciprocal obligations according to the *adat*.[27] To live on land means being in a relationship with other people who live on the same land.

Houses were built in two parallel positions facing each other with the existence of shared public space in the middle for public use. In this shared space, the community dried their harvested rice and did weaving or carpentry. Kids would play, and teenagers would learn traditional dance in this space. It was also a space for *adat* ceremonies, public announcements, court proceedings, and general socialization. The community law (*adat*) divides the areas in the *huta* in to private or communal/public use. *Adat* categorizes each space depending on its use and people's needs. *Adat* regulates the allocation of land, the arrangement of houses, the establishment of shared space, and the formation of prohibited space. With this role of *adat*, every space is at once a political, economic, religious, and cultural space with no strict boundaries, as all these aspects interconnect with each other to define the social matrix of space. This condition is precisely why reciprocal relationships and a holistic approach to social life are possible.

The people's social identity was constructed in that it was closely connected to the land they inhabited and inherited from one generation to the next. Losing a piece of land means losing one's social position in society. The identity explained here refers not only to family, social, and cultural aspects but also to economic and religious dimensions. Living on the land has already included a sense of interdependence on the life-giving aspects of nature, rice fields, farms, and forests. For that reason, economic activities were conducted in sustainable ways. More importantly, economic pursuits were not driven by self-interest, wealth accumulation, or greed. Instead, the goal was to preserve families in the village so that all people could flourish and maintain their well-being together. For this reason, the Batak people would leave some spaces unoccupied. Some forests were left untouched as a space for preservation, while others could be utilized for limited purposes only after the village made a communal decision.[28]

This awareness came along when the Batak people realized that soil was sacred. Simanjuntak points out that in Batak mythology, the God

Creator called *Debata Mulajadi Nabolon* gave a piece of soil to *Si Boru Deak Parujar*—the goddess of harvest and blessings—which became the beginning of the earth. This all started when *Si Boru Deak Parujar*, *Batara Guru*'s daughter, was forced by her father to enter into an arranged marriage with *Siraja Odapodap*, Mangala Bulan's son, whom she did not love. She fled the upper world through a spun thread to the dark and watery middle world. She did not have a place to set her feet on. Upon her request, *Debata Mulajadi Nabolon* sent a piece of soil that she spread out on the head of *Naga Pahoda*, the underworld dragon.

The dragon kept rolling and threatened to destroy the newly created earth, but *Si Boru Deak Parujar* protected the earth by sticking a sword to the dragon's body and putting him in an iron block. Humans were born from the marriage of *Si Boru Deak Parujar* with *Siraja Odapodap*, who came to the earth with another name and form.[29] This mythology tells that the earth was created as divine grace and protected by the goddess. The Batak bear sacred traces as they were born of a god and a goddess. With these theological background in mind, the Batak people believed it was necessary to seek God's blessings before they could start a *huta*. Starting a *huta* was considered a religious act. Before a Batak community could initiate a village, their leaders had to place offerings on the new land and leave them for one night. A shaman would determine if the offerings showed signs of blessings. If so, there would be one to three weeks of waiting (taboo) period before they could enter and start building houses. Usually, the best location for a new village would be at the foot of a mountain. The people believed such a location would bring health and blessings to the community.[30]

The Batak people believed that every space had its own spiritual occupant, so they should treat every space with respect for divine blessings to materialize. Soil and land could not be treated as merely a tool for economic fulfillment. Forests could not be exploited irresponsibly. People had to conduct religious rituals before taking wood from the forest, and only selective wood was allowed to be taken. Trees around a water source, such as a lake, could not be cut down.[31] It is evident that the Batak people's concerns with ecological sustainability were closely entwined with their understanding of God, religion, and community. Ecology and the economy come together to meet the people's basic needs. Despite embodying the subsistence economy, the people understand subsistence as a means to provide enough for every human in the community.

THE NEW THEOLOGY OF THE LAND:
THE COLONIAL AND NEO-COLONIAL ERA

When Christianity first came to Batakland in 1861, the Dutch colonizers had not yet annexed the region. Therefore, the missionaries were independent of Dutch colonial powers as they began the work of evangelizing. The European missionaries, who were part of the Rheinische Missionsgesellschaft (RMG), of which the most well-known was Ingwer Ludwig Nommensen, were interested in saving the "lost souls" of the Batak people by converting them to the new religion. They sought to transform Batak society in general, but they did it in ways that imitated the European concept of the separation of state and church. According to Sita van Bemmelen, this transformation separated ancestral worship and rituals (religion) from customs (*adat*). The missionaries would reject ancestral worship and maintain traditional customs.[32] These efforts led to the rejection of the indigenous religion in general and the loss of indigenous wisdom that was immediately connected to the indigenous theology and customs on the land. Since the Batak people believed that the land was gifted by the goddess *Si Boru Deak Parujar* and that spirits inhabit the land, the belief was considered to be opposed to Christianity and, therefore, had to be rejected. Missionaries, hence, contributed at the spiritual level in which the indigenous theology of the land was removed from the lived experience of the people.

The Batak mission introduced a theology of salvation that did not correspond with a holistic salvation concept that included the environment. The land, thus, was left out of the conversation about faith and salvation. The social-theological background is because the Batak mission carried with it the spirit of pietism that looked at reality in dichotomic ways. Salvation addresses the soul or spirit, while the body is not essential to human salvation. Jan Aritonang discusses how the theological education taught at RMG seminary was influenced by the pietistic and revivalist movements that centralized one's personal relationship with God and individual salvation.[33] J. C. Wallmann (1811–1865), who taught at the RMG seminary in Barmen, promoted "a theology of redemption originating out of the revival movement."[34] He considered indigenous religions to be pagan and entities to which the light should come to chase away the darkness. G. L. von Rohden (1817–1889), the longest-serving teacher under whom many Batak mission missionaries studied, held a view of the Germans as divinely-elected "protector and maintainer of the divine treasury of grace."[35] He was also a supporter of German national-Protestantism. Racist RMG missionaries brought this model of theology to their mission work. F. G. K. E. Fabri (1824–1891), the most influential teacher, viewed that the Christian mission works "to communicate the Gospel from the white race, including Germanic peoples, to the dark-skinned pagans, and at the same time to spread a higher civilization."[36] He thought that the government and mission should work together and later forced German Chancellor Bismarck to support evangelization.[37] The conclusion is that most, if not all, Barmen seminary teachers held a revivalist, nationalist, and racist theology that missionaries brought with them when they arrived in Batakland.

When the Dutch colonizers annexed Batakland, the theology of the land started to change drastically. The Batak people's encounter with Western culture and Dutch colonization turned the once free Batak lands into plantations. Uli Kozok notes that in the Mandailing area, the colonizer forced the people to grow coffee and sell it to them at a fixed price.[38] In Karo and Simalungun, the people lost the rights to their land as the plantation economy took over. Thousands of coolies, many of whom were of Chinese descent, were transported from the Malay peninsula and Java to work on the plantations. This led to a rapid population increase that also increased demand for food. The Toba Batak people, knowledgeable in irrigated rice-field systems, immigrated to surrounding areas, especially lands distributed by the colonial government, to work and cultivate food.[39] In the Toba Batak areas, the people followed the Europeans' lead as they started to grow rubber on a large scale. Kozok notes that between 1921 and 1927, rubber production grew from 204 to almost 5,000 tons.[40] As the subsistence economy declined, the land was transformed to serve the market economy and devoted to growing and exporting commodities like vegetables, fruit, coffee, and cloves. More significantly, industrialized plantations became more prevalent as rubber, palm oil, cocoa, and tea became increasingly valuable commodities. Using fertilizers and massive deforestation was inevitable, leading to ecological destruction.[41]

At the political level, unlike other colonial contexts, the justification for colonial occupation of the land did not reflect the characteristics of the "terra nullius" (nobody's land) doctrine. Instead, the land occupation was justified through a series of codifications called the "Domain Verklarin" doctrine and the existing feudalism system. The doctrine states, "all lands without having a proof of its legality are owned by the State." As the native chiefs or kings were forced to acknowledge the Dutch colonizers as their new "landlord" following their defeat or surrender, the previously unrecognized concept of land legality in the indigenous culture became the justification for the colonial seizure of their land. In this way, the Dutch colonial government claimed all territories and stripped the indigenous people of their collective relationships with their land. The Dutch colonizers imposed different laws derived from the civil and commercial laws of the Netherlands known as the "Concordance Principle." They implemented a land tax system that treated indigenous people as renters, adopted a monopoly system, and forced the implementation of cultivation systems (*Cultuurstelstel*) to protect their economic goals.[42] The indigenous theology of the land was replaced with the colonial concepts of private ownership, legal territory, and commodified land.

At theological and cultural levels, the colonial government imposed on the people the desire for advancement (*hamajuon*). Jan Aritonang notes that the modern Western culture that penetrated the Batak culture contributed to the way the Batak people saw the material world. The spirit of *hamajuon* came along with the colonial economic development projects mentioned above. The introduction of communication and transportation facilities by the colonial government brought access to Western material culture, including recreation: movie houses, billiards, dance halls, gambling games, bars, and bordellos. Young people were motivated to leave their ancestral land to seek material improvement.[43] Later development shows that the desire for material wealth drove some Bataks to sell their ancestral lands and emigrate to big cities to pursue their passion for upward economic mobility. For some, the land became a tool to serve their material pursuits.

The postcolonial government is not any different in its treatment of indigenous land. Herman Hidayat et al. have traced the historical development of Indonesia's forests in relation to Indonesian indigenous communities. They concluded that the acquisition of indigenous land during the colonial era continued after independence in 1945. The central government remains in control of forests in different parts of Indonesia, which has resulted in the loss of customary forests in Batakland. The colonial 1865 Forest Law that stipulates that forests are under the control of the State remains in effect. In the authoritarian New Order era, the government controlled income-producing forests through the legislation of the Mining Law 11/1968 and Basic Forestry Law 5/1967. These laws allowed for the exploitation of natural resources. After the fall of the New Order regime in 1998, the central government issued the Forestry Law 1999, the Mining and Mineral Law 2009, and the Local Government Law 2014, laws that continue to thwart indigenous peoples' control over their land.[44] In different Batak regions, colonial attitudes that deemed land a commodity persist. In cooperation with the central government, private companies have acquired massive tracts of land for large-scale production that destroys the environment. Forests that used to be considered sacred and full of divine traces that sustain diverse entities have been turned into monolithic commodities. Conflicts of land between the people and the government have become inevitable and increasingly common.

This postcolonial reality reflects more than the construction of "anthropocentric land," in which land is ultimately seen as a commodity to serve human interest. Further, it demonstrates the formation of neoliberal reasoning by which all spheres of life are transformed to meet economic principles. For this reason, colonialism persists in a new form called neo-colonialism that does not necessarily depend on territorial occupation but political control from the center of power through neoliberal rationality. The Indonesian postcolonial government falls into this trap of neoliberal reasoning. On neoliberalism, Michel Foucault has called this rational restructuring "neoliberal governmentality,"[45] which is the general art of governing that takes on the principles of the market.[46] This style of governance facilitates economic models in which all aspects of life submit to the ultimate goal of economic growth. Drawing on Foucault, Wendy Brown views the economization of all domains of life as threatening the basic principles of democracy because it shapes democratic subjects into economic subjects alone (*homo oeconomicus*).[47] Initially concerned with the public good, political life reduces its goal to "economic growth, global competitiveness, and maintenance of a strong credit rating."[48] This relates to theologies of the land in how colonial and neocolonial forces remove indigenous theology and construct a colonial theology of anthropocentric land. It also involves the transformation of the theological anthropology of indigenous subjects, altering them into economic subjects alone who define religion, *adat*, relationships, social status, prestige, and nature based on their economic purposes and profitability.[49]

COMPARING THE BATAK AND THE POST/COLONIAL THEOLOGIES

From the exploration above, we can compare Batak theology and colonial theology about the land. The Batak theology of the land centers around the human relationship with other human beings, the divine, and the environment. This conception is derived from the customary law (*adat*) that inspires and infuses every dimension of life. Human relationships with the land are ecological as much as they are religious, social, cultural, economic, and political. The land is sacred, and the use of different types of land respects its sacred dimension and correlates with how the community is well-sustained and nature is preserved. The Batak's lived experience of their indigenous land extends beyond their verbal acknowledgment or theological reasoning of its sacredness. It operates within their religious rituals, village planning, community building, and economic activities.

From the conversion of most Batak people to Christianity and the imposition of Western modernity, the ecologically friendly and spiritual conception of land has turned into an "anthropocentric land," contributing to land conflicts, land commodification, and ecological destruction. Colonial and neocolonial theology turns land into commodities. The land loses its ecological dimension as it serves solely economic purposes. Colonial theology overturns the land's communal aspects as the land becomes privatized and individualized. It defines land as individual property and signifier of wealth based on legal justifications. This theology inherited from the colonial era continues today in ways that not only transform human relationships with the land but also with the divine, the human other, and the environment.

However, comparing both theologies in their historical development rejects an easy fix of the either/or conclusion. For the precolonial Batak, the culture of the land was highly patriarchal, and this mostly continues today. The Batak theology of the land has not allowed much space for women. The tradition of passing land down through inheritance mainly benefits men. After marriage, a Batak woman joins her husband's family, which ties her to the inherited land of her husband, rather than that of her family's. Only sons are culturally eligible to inherit land. Parents can give their daughters a piece of land as a gift but not as an inheritance. This gift is called *pauseang*, a rice field gifted to a married daughter, intended to help her new family economically.[50] Since these distributions are gifts, there is no guarantee that parents (especially if they are relatively poor) will allocate it to their daughters. The coming of Christianity, on the other hand, has contributed to more equal conditions. Churches have advocated for more equal rights for women, including the right to inherit land. Conditions have not changed drastically, but some Batak parents have become more open to distributing the land as an inheritance to their daughters, sometimes in equal shares and sometimes with smaller portions.

Hence, Walter Mignolo and Catherine Walsh's analysis of coloniality as the colonial matrix of power in modernity may not give a sufficient explanation of the theologies of the land.[51] The colonial matrix of power in this imposed theology of land amalgamates European colonization, Christian mission, European modernity, racism, capitalism, and the internalized colonization of the postcolonial government together. These are the configurations of power at work that have and continue to strip the Batak people of their indigenous theology of the land. But the colonial element as discriminatory treatment of particular segments of the society can also be found in an indigenous culture itself. Comparing the precolonial, colonial, and postcolonial theologies of the land in the Batak community suggests that comparative theologies of the land as lived experience cannot be seen as "merely texts" but "living traditions" that become parts of mundane interaction, constant interrogation, and complicated negotiation. The historical matrix of colonial power shapes how theologies of land are constructed, shaped, believed, and lived through practices impacting the multidimensionality and plurality of life throughout history. Considering this multidimensionality, postcolonial comparative theologies of the land must recognize "the colonial" as more than an epistemological problem. The colonial goes beyond coloniality—that is, the logic of the colonial characterized by knowledge production and its content. The colonial also includes the frameworks and structures of oppression and practices of domination that are concretized in practical manifestations.

COMPARATIVE REFLECTIVITY AND INTERFAITH ENGAGEMENT

If comparative theology pays attention to the texture of people's lived experiences and the configuration of power in compared theologies, it can offer more than a learning process centered on cognition. Comparative theology becomes the process of affective and psychomotor interreligious learning as a praxis of remembering, reimagining, revaluing, relearning, and re-acting to lost indigenous theologies and practices that are life-giving and nurturing. This approach can be called "comparative reflectivity," in which theological comparison is situated within the community as a praxis of continuous reflection and action. In this comparative reflectivity, the Batak community is enabled to embrace the hybridity and complexity of their postcolonial reality. Reflectivity refers to the ability to remember, reinvent, and recollect the memories and past wisdom of their lost indigenous heritage and perform rituals accordingly. This capacity reaches its fullest potential when they truthfully compare their past experience and relationships with their ancestral land to shed light on their present relationships with the land.

Najeeba Syeed's response to comparative theology is essential in this process. Syeed argues that comparative theology should not function only to acknowledge the "appreciative inquiry" and "theologies of cooperation" potential comparative theologies have brought but must also identify how one religion can be the source of oppression for another and to transparently expose the "theology of domination" and the "theology of the dominated." Syeed continues, "when one tradition is the source of oppression for another, we must hear how the targeted community articulates and experiences the theologies of domination of our own."[52] Since such a comparative theology does not assume or occupy an isolated space or neutral ground, interreligious learning becomes the praxis of remembering the past, embracing the present, and envisioning the future—a process filled with change, messiness, and transformation. Interreligious learning can benefit from recognizing the messiness of the historical development of a theological conception and the subjective experience of a community. The purpose is to bring liberation to the community that lives the theology mentioned above.

When the Batak community engages in comparative reflectivity, they are invited to identify the dominated theology of the land, recognize its strengths and limitations, and reinvigorate it as a renewal theology that can challenge the colonial matrix of power. Recognizing its limitations is an important aspect of this process since not all aspects of indigenous wisdom contain a liberating impulse. Kwok Pui-lan anticipates this condition by suggesting that using indigenous wisdom does not mean finding pure native theologies but transcending the past and the present by evaluating the past.[53] In practical terms, the Batak community can and should not use their indigenous theology of the land to evoke identity politics of pure nativity but rather to reinvent the liberatory principles and practices of the past and apply them to contemporary struggles. Evaluating a dominated theology with comparative reflectivity requires critical analysis that includes the oppressed others of the precolonial era. The story of *Si Boru Deak Parujar* offers an example of a way to amplify women's agency against normative, patriarchal rules and protect their rights to life and land in line with the preservation of the earth. Women's courage to fight against the patriarchal system corresponds directly to the creation and protection of the land. The Goddess can inspire women's liberative actions for their unwavering self-determination and emancipation, a vital resource worth reflecting on.

For Batak Christians, honoring indigenous wisdom can help construct a contextual theology that resists the hegemony of white Western Christianity and other forms of globalized Christianity and, therefore, can become a tool for decolonizing hegemonic/colonial Christianity. Constructing a contextual theology may, in turn, facilitate the formation of local Christianities that respect and learn from indigenous traditions. This process can lead to the formation of a hybrid Christianity that engages with local culture, theology, and social expression. More importantly, by learning from indigenous traditions, local Christianity can return to tradition and excavate forgotten Christian resources—in this case, ones related to the land's theology—to find some principal resonances and liberating voices. These newly discovered resources may turn out to be very different from the normative biblical and theological interpretations that white Christian scholars offer. Being faithful to both traditions—their indigenous roots and Christianity—the Batak Christians may hold to their true integrity as they engage both faithfully without undermining one another. This engagement reflects what Rita Nakashima Brock calls "interstitial integrity," the integrity of life that faithfully holds to but critically struggles with the many identities. Interstitial integrity, Brock writes, "helps us to be attuned to the fullness of life, to appreciate its many pleasures, and to participate in its ever-changing rhythms and patterns, rather than to be starved by unrealized hopes or a thin nostalgic past."[54]

Comparative reflectivity also corresponds to emphasizing the need for interfaith engagement. Comparative theology can elevate minoritized religious traditions by comparing two religious traditions lived within one ethnic community wherein there remain people who practice indigenous traditions without associating themselves with the dominant religious tradition. In the Batak context, some who call themselves *Parmalim* still practice indigenous religion and do not identify themselves as Christians, but they are often oppressed. Recognizing their existence calls for interfaith engagement that values comparative theology as "a form of allyship," as Syeed suggests. We can have a sense of belonging to our traditions, but we also need to be radical allies to marginalized people.[55] This radical allyship is possible when one appreciates theologies, especially dominated theologies, as more than texts but living traditions practiced by real people. By bringing minoritized traditions into comparative theology, interfaith engagement not only destabilizes the World Religions paradigm but also redirects focus to the fact that dominated theologies often belong to dominated people.

NOTES

1. Hedges, "Theorising a Decolonising Asian Hermeneutic," 153. What Hedges means by the potential of comparative theology here reflects on its emphasis to cross "borders [between religious traditions] and return to a home tradition to renew it."
2. Hedges, "Theorising a Decolonising Asian Hermeneutic," 155–56.
3. Masuzawa, *The Invention of World Religions*, 3. The classification of great religions, according to Masuzawa, includes three categories based on geographic origin: ancient Near East (Judaism, Christianity, Islam), South Asia (Hinduism, Buddhism, Zoroastrianism, Jainism), and the Far East (Confucianism, Taoism, Shinto). This categorization is consonant with the comparative philology of the nineteenth century that posited three groups of languages: Semitic (or Hamito-Semitic), Aryan (or Indo-European), and Turanian (or Oriental).
4. Masuzawa, *The Invention of World Religions*, 4.
5. Christianity, Islam, Judaism, Hinduism, and Buddhism. This list can be extended to include Confucianism, Taoism, and Shintoism.
6. Tiemeier, "Comparative Theology as a Theology of Liberation," 140.
7. Marianne Moyaert proposes including "material and ritual practices" in doing comparative theology, in addition to and to complement textual sources. She calls this method "liturgical comparative theology." See Moyaert, "Towards a Ritual Turn."
8. Asad, *Genealogies of Religion*, 29. I continue to use the word "religion" interchangeably with "tradition." Rather than semantics, I am more focused on how power shapes religions, traditions, or theologies.
9. Foucault, *Discipline and Punish*, 27.
10. In this essay, I use "postcoloniality" and "decoloniality" interchangeably, despite their different methodologies, to emphasize that both theories emerged from the context of colonization, which this essay seeks to address.
11. Foucault, *Discipline and Punish*, 137.
12. Quijano, "Coloniality of Power."
13. Mignolo and Walsh, *On Decoloniality*, 114.
14. Said, *Orientalism*, 5.

15. Hall, "When Was 'the Post-Colonial'?," 254.
16. Chung, *Comparative Theology*, 285.
17. Tiemeier, "Comparative Theology as a Theology of Liberation," 138.
18. Knott, *The Location of Religion*, 3.
19. Knott, *The Location of Religion*, 21.
20. Clooney, *Comparative Theology*, 11.
21. I am indebted to Homi Bhabha's use of the word "hybridity" as in-between reality, the difference "within." See Bhabha, *The Location of Culture*, 13.
22. The literal meaning is "the Great Creator" or "the Great Creator of all that exists."
23. Sinaga, *Allah Tinggi Batak-Toba*, 47–49.
24. Sinaga, *Allah Tinggi Batak*-Toba, 55.
25. Sinaga, *Allah Tinggi Batak-Toba*, 88–90. Ancestor spirits are believed to occupy the land of the dead, which allows them to interact with the living.
26. Simanjuntak, *Arti dan Fungsi Tanah*, 21–24.
27. Sibeth, *The Batak*, 46.
28. Simanjuntak, *Arti dan Fungsi Tanah*, 37.
29. A short version of the myth can be found in Sibeth, *The Batak*, 65.
30. Simanjuntak, *Arti dan Fungsi Tanah*, 36.
31. Simanjuntak, *Arti dan Fungsi Tanah*, 37–38.
32. van Bemmelen, *Christianity, Colonization, and Gender*, 230.
33. Aritonang and Steenbrink, *A History of Christianity*, 537.
34. Aritonang, *Mission Schools in Batakland*, 71.
35. Aritonang, *Mission Schools in Batakland*, 73.
36. Aritonang, *Mission Schools in Batakland*, 75.
37. Aritonang, *Mission Schools in Batakland*, 70–89. One seminary teacher named Gustav Warneck (1834–1910) had a more open theology and attitude toward indigenous religions. Although he believed that Christianity was the only religion that could offer life, he believed other religions, including paganism, inherited the *logos spermatikos*, the seed of the gospel or the spark by which life may be found. This seed of life, though, is not strong enough for people to reach eternal life.
38. Kozok, "The Economic Foundation," 31-38.
39. Kozok, "The Economic Foundation," 31–38.
40. Kozok, "The Economic Foundation," 36.
41. Kozok, "The Economic Foundation," 37–38.
42. For more details on the different systems the colonial government enforced, see Fahmi, "The Dutch Colonial Economic's Policy."
43. Aritonang, *Mission Schools in Batakland*, 230. Aritonang notes that the missionaries were rather hostile to these kinds of Western culture. They thought it would not bring good to the society as it would result in "impoverishment, addiction and ultimately destruction of its life" and render the mission work would become useless. Instead, they focused more on *hamajuon partondion*

(spiritual advancement) and worked to promote it as an important foundation for external/material advancement.
44. Hidayat et al., "Forests, Law and Customary Rights," 297–98. For more on the Indonesian indigenous rights to their customary forests, see my presentation entitled "Decolonizing Customary Forests: The Struggle of Indigenous Groups for Land Rights in Indonesia."
45. Foucault, *The Birth of Biopolitics*, 192.
46. Foucault, *The Birth of Biopolitics,* 131.
47. Brown, *Undoing the Demos*.
48. Brown, *Undoing the Demos*, 39–40.
49. One example of how economic principles materialize in Batak churches is the common practice of auctioning in religious festivals to do fundraising. Batara Sihombing has discussed and criticized this practice as "less justifiable as a church fund-raising activity." Sihombing connects this practice to one of the three Batak ideals *hamoraon* (riches) and asserts that it is not a practice introduced by the RMG missionaries. Although we can immediately identify the practice of auctioning as an economic practice in the religious setting, Sihombing's analysis could be furthered by paying attention to the historical background and recognizing that the formation of Batak subjects was intensely influenced by the spirit of *hamajuon* as derived from the encounter with the Western culture and Dutch colonization. As a concept, *hamoraon* may be best understood not as a static idea but as an evolving one undergoing change throughout time. Sihombing, "Mission for the Practice of Auction," 376–85.
50. Simanjuntak, *Arti dan Fungsi*, 25–26.
51. Mignolo and Walsh further claim that modernity engenders coloniality, and that there cannot be modernity without coloniality. To abolish coloniality would mean terminating the fiction of modernity.
52. Syeed, "Interreligious Learning and Intersectionality," 177.
53. Kwok, *Postcolonial Imagination*, 69.
54. Brock, "Cooking without Recipes," 139.
55. Syeed, "Interreligious Learning and Intersectionality," 177.

REFERENCES

Aritonang, Jan S. *Mission Schools in Batakland (Indonesia): 1861–1940*. Translated by Robert R. Boehlke. Leiden: Brill, 1994.

Aritonang, Jan S., and Karel A. Steenbrink, eds. *A History of Christianity in Indonesia*. Studies in Christian Mission, v. 35. Leiden: Brill, 2008.

Asad, Talal. *Genealogies of Religion: Discipline and Reasons of Power in Christianity and Islam*. Baltimore: Johns Hopkins University Press, 1993.

Bemmelen, Sita van. *Christianity, Colonization, and Gender Relations in North Sumatra: A Patrilineal Society in Flux*. Verhandelingen van Het Koninklijk Instituut Voor Taal-, Land- En Volkenkunde, volume 309. Leiden: Brill, 2018.

Bhabha, Homi K. *The Location of Culture*. London: Routledge, 1994.

Brock, Rita Nakashima. "Cooking without Recipes: Interstitial Integrity." In *Off the Menu: Asian and Asian North American Women's Religion and Theology*, edited by Rita Nakashima Brock, Jung Ha Kim, Pui-lan Kwok, and Seung Ai Yang, 125–43. Louisville, KY: Westminster John Knox, 2007.

Brown, Wendy. *Undoing the Demos: Neoliberalism's Stealth Revolution*. New York: Zone Books, 2015.

Chung, Paul S. *Comparative Theology Among Multiple Modernities: Cultivating Phenomenological Imagination*. Cham: Springer International, 2017. https://doi.org/10.1007/978-3-319-58196-5.

Clooney, Francis X. *Comparative Theology: Deep Learning Across Religious Borders*. Malden, MA: Wiley-Blackwell, 2010.

Fahmi, Chairul. "The Dutch Colonial Economic's Policy on Natives Land Property of Indonesia." *PETITA: Jurnal Kajian Ilmu Hukum dan Syariah* 5, no. 2 (November 1, 2020), 105–120. https://doi.org/10.22373/petita.v5i2.99.

Foucault, Michel. *Discipline and Punish: The Birth of Prison*. Translated by Alan Sheridan. New York: Vintage Books, 1977.

Foucault, Michel. *The Birth of Biopolitics: Lectures at the Collège de France, 1978–79*. Edited by Michel Senellart. New York: Palgrave Macmillan, 2008.

Hall, Stuart. "When Was 'the Post-Colonial'? Thinking at the Limit." In *The Postcolonial Question: Common Skies, Divided Horizons*, edited by Iain Chambers and Lidia Curti, 242–60. London and New York: Routledge, 1995.

Hedges, Paul. "Theorising a Decolonising Asian Hermeneutic for Comparative Theology: Some Perspectives from Global and Singaporean Eyes." *International Journal of Asian Christianity* 3, no. 2 (September 3, 2020): 152–68. https://doi.org/10.1163/25424246-00302004.

Hidayat, Herman, Herry Yogaswara, Tuti Herawati, Patricia Blazey, Stephen Wyatt, and Richard Howitt. "Forests, Law and Customary Rights in Indonesia: Implications of a Decision of the Indonesian Constitutional Court in 2012." *Asia Pacific Viewpoint* 59, no. 3 (December 2018): 293–308. https://doi.org/10.1111/apv.12207.

Knott, Kim. *The Location of Religion: A Spatial Analysis*. London: Equinox, 2005.

Kozok, Uli. "The Economic Foundation of the Society." In *The Batak: Peoples of the Island of Sumatra*, by Achim Sibeth, 31–38. New York: Thames and Hudson, 1991.

Kwok, Pui-lan. *Postcolonial Imagination and Feminist Theology*. Louisville: Westminster John Knox, 2005.

Masuzawa, Tomoko. *The Invention of World Religions, or, How European Universalism Was Preserved in the Language of Pluralism*. Chicago: University of Chicago Press, 2005.

Mignolo, Walter D., and Catherine E. Walsh. *On Decoloniality: Concepts, Analytics, Praxis*. Durham, NC: Duke University Press, 2018.

Moyaert, Marianne. "Towards a Ritual Turn in Comparative Theology: Opportunities, Challenges, and Problems." *Harvard Theological Review* 111, no. 1 (January 2018): 1–23, https://doi.org/10.1017/S0017816017000360.

Quijano, Anibal. "Coloniality of Power, Eurocentrism, and Latin America." Translated by Michael Ennis. *Nepantla: Views from South* 1, no. 3 (2000): 533–80. https://doi.org/10.1177/026858090001500 2005.

Said, Edward W. *Orientalism*. New York: Vintage Books, 1978.

Sibeth, Achim. *The Batak: Peoples of the Island of Sumatra*. New York: Thames and Hudson, 1991.

Sihombing, Batara. "Mission for the Practice of Auction in the Batak Church in Indonesia." *Exchange* 34, no. 4 (2005): 376–85. https://doi.org/10.1163/1572 54305774851529.

Sihombing, Hesron. "Decolonizing Customary Forests: The Struggle of Indigenous Groups for Land Rights in Indonesia" Presented at *Christian Left Conference 2022, Emmanuel College, Toronto (online), August 5–6, 2022*.

Simanjuntak, Bungaran Antonius. *Arti dan Fungsi Tanah Bagi Masyarakat Batak Toba, Karo, Simalungun (Edisi Pembaruan)*. Jakarta: Yayasan Pustaka Obor Indonesia, 2015.

Sinaga, Anicetus B. *Allah Tinggi Batak-Toba*. Yogyakarta: Kanisius, 2014.

Syeed, Najeeba. "Interreligious Learning and Intersectionality." In *Asian and Asian American Women in Theology and Religion: Embodying Knowledge*, edited by Pui-lan Kwok, 171–85. Asian Christianity in the Diaspora. Cham: Palgrave Macmillan, 2020. https://doi.org/10.1007/978-3-030-36818-0.

Tiemeier, Tracy Sayuki. "Comparative Theology as a Theology of Liberation." In *The New Comparative Theology: Interreligious Insights From the Next Generation*, edited by Francis X. Clooney, 129–49. London: T & T Clark, 2010.

MICHELLE VOSS ROBERTS

SPIRIT(S) AND THE LAND

A Comparative Theological Exploration of Two Contemporary Indigenous Visions

When I moved to Canada in 2018, I began to hear, both from Indigenous colleagues and in regular land acknowledgements, about the importance of the land. Though intrigued and appreciative, I recognized that the importance of the land escaped my categories. Land acknowledgements recognize the people on whose traditional territories I live and work, and they remind me that I am a settler and a guest here. But that is not all. These statements profess a relation to the land, which includes ecological responsibility, that I also believe to be important. That, too, is not all. When Indigenous people talk about the power of being "on the land," what they mean seems to exceed my appreciation of wonder and beauty in "nature." The land is sacred in ways I cannot quite comprehend. And I also confess to being at a loss to comprehend the claim of the Sandy-Saulteaux Spiritual Centre (the Indigenous ministry training school of my denomination, the United Church of Canada) that "The Earth is Our Faculty."[1] What does it mean to learn from the land? For land to be a teacher? For land to exercise agency in relation to us? And what is the theological status of this land, professed to be both sacred and agential?

The Indigenous theologians encountered in this article identify *spirit* as the source of the land's agency. Land is not only sacred but *enspirited*. As animate, land does not refer only to soil and territory, but to all animate beings on it. Anishinaabe legal scholar John Borrows explains of his land-based pedagogy, "When I speak of land, I am also speaking of all the natural phenomena associated with the land, such as water."[2] Learning from the land entails attention to the wisdom of the caribou nation, the salmon, the coyote. However, from the perspective of colonial interpretations of Christian tradition, the prospect of spirit in the land raises red flags. The dominant tradition has fought mightily to remove any hint of polytheism, pantheism, or other "isms" that would position divinity too close to the material world. Confronting this knee-jerk reaction to possible "heresy" in land-based theologizing is imperative. This is part of the decolonization of theological studies, which involves the self-definition of people and communities who have lived close to the land and have been subject to assimilation by colonizing powers.

It is easy for settlers asking questions about the land's status and importance to go astray. Vanessa Watts alleges that people schooled in Western thought quickly depart from the Indigenous teachings about the land from which we profess to want to learn. We have an intellectual habit of severing epistemology from ontology. "From a theoretical standpoint," she writes, "the material (body/land) becomes abstracted into epistemological spaces as a resource for non-Indigenous scholars to implode their hegemonic borders."[3] Western thinkers tend to want an abstract intellectual sandbox. We want a *lesson to take away*, without transforming our understanding of reality. And in doing so, we replicate the extractive patterns that settler colonizers have enacted toward Indigenous people and the land for hundreds of years on Turtle Island.

As a White Christian settler theologian, I hear Watts calling upon me to treat the enspirited character of the land as an ontological question. In my academic discipline and teaching context, an ontological question is also a *theological* question. In the Jewish and Christian traditions, God self-reveals with the name "I am who I am" or "I will be who I will be" (Exodus 3:14). Christian theologians tend to think of divinity as the very *being* or *becoming* of everything that is. At the same time, I must acknowledge that some Indigenous thinkers would dispute that *theology* is an appropriate framework at all. Those who follow the traditional ways of their communities may view theology or philosophy as a colonial imposition. Others, whether following Christian or traditional Indigenous ways, might simply experience theological questions about the land as foreign to the community's ways of speaking and knowing. They might understand the land in relation to their way of being but would avoid concretizing the metaphysics of this relationship. Such understandings would, in any case, differ from nation to nation and from person to person and could not be generalized.[4] However, other Christian thinkers from Indigenous communities, including those considered in this essay, argue for the theological legitimacy of their ways of being in relationship to the land, which Christian missionaries and theologians have denigrated. Chastened by these different perspectives, this work of comparative theology attempts to learn in a limited fashion from two exemplars of the latter approach, for whom the being and becoming of the land matters for discourse about the divine: Alf Dumont (Anishinaabe) and Keneipfenuo Rüpreo Angami (Naga).

CONTEXT AND INTERLOCUTORS

I am exploring the theological status of the land in the works of Indigenous theologians from two different contexts at a time when comparative theologians are being called to decolonize our discipline. Tracy Sayuki Tiemeier, a Japanese-German American theologian working in Los Angeles, has been a leading proponent of comparative work that is liberative, anti-racist, and decolonial. Drawing on Khyati Joshi's important analysis of Christian norms in American life, Tiemeier asks her fellow theologians to learn about interreligious issues, prioritize the concerns and categories of other communities, and "[privilege] minoritized traditions and sources on all sides of the comparison."[5] In this spirit, the following study amplifies the voices of two Indigenous Christian theologians, one from Turtle Island and one from India, to understand a matter of importance in each of their writings: the enspirited quality of the land.

I also undertake this exploration in a particular place and time. The nation known as Canada overlaps with the traditional territories of many First Nation, Métis, and Inuit people. A complex history and ongoing negotiations have resulted in a situation in which many Canadians live on unceded territories, others reside on land covered by treaties that have been only partially honored, some Indigenous people live on lands set aside as reserves, and in some places the nations are rediscovering modes of joint stewardship and governance. Christian churches were complicit in the Canadian government's policies of cultural genocide by administering residential "schools" that removed Indigenous children from their lands and territories and often subjected them to abuse. In 2015, the Truth and Reconciliation Commission issued 94 Calls to Action exhorting every level of the Canadian government "to redress the legacy of residential schools and advance the process of Canadian reconciliation."[6] This context impacts the questions I ask and the teachers of whom I ask them.

Reverend Alf Dumont is an Anishinaabe (Ojibwe) minister and spiritual leader from the land near where I live and work in Ontario, Canada. He is a leading Indigenous figure in my denomination, the United Church of Canada, and an alumnus of the theological school where I teach. His work is a natural choice for me as a comparative theologian writing in southern Ontario, as I attempt, as John Borrows advises, to "pay attention to the Indigenous nations around [me], even in urban settings."[7]

Dumont grew up on "both sides of the river," on the land now called Shawanaga First Nation.[8] The river's two sides provide the animating metaphor of his memoir, *The Other Side of the River: From Church Pew to Sweat Lodge*, which explores his dual heritage of Christian and traditional Anishinaabe spiritualities. He was the first director of the Dr. Jessie Saulteaux Resource Centre in Saskatchewan, which is the predecessor to the current Sandy-Saulteaux Spiritual Centre in Beausejour, Manitoba. It was founded "to have First Nations people train for ministry and then serve in their own communities."[9] Dumont has had a major role in forming the ethos of the United Church of Canada concerning Indigenous-settler relations. In addition to being the founding director of the Centre, he was instrumental to the formation of the All Native Circle Conference in the denomination. Serving as the Circle's first Speaker, he guided their response when the United Church apologized for not respecting the spiritual and cultural ways of the first peoples of the land. He is currently an elder at the Indigenous Centre at the British Columbia Institute of Technology.

Keneipfenuo Rüpreo Angami is a tribal (Angami Naga) Christian theologian from Nagaland, one of the eight states in the eastern range of the Himalayas, in what is known in colonial terms as Northeast India. The people of this region traditionally practiced "primal religions," which, though diverse in relation to one another, are based in the rhythms of the natural world rather than texts or built structures, and which perceive the world non-dichotomously and permeated with spirits. While Hindus are prominent on the plains of these states, alongside Muslims and Buddhists, the hill regions have had a high majority of Christians in the tribal population since the arrival of the Christian missionaries in the nineteenth century. The groups that live in the Northeastern states are, therefore, extraordinarily linguistically, ethnically, culturally, and religiously diverse.[10] This region was under British rule from 1826–1947, creating a buffer between India and neighboring countries.

Neocolonial rule by India began with Indian independence, which inaugurated a period in the Northeastern states characterized by isolation, Indian military rule, and the decentralized forces of global capitalism. As Angami describes the colonial situation,

> [The] arbitrary demarcation of the Northeast region created chaos among the local people, accentuating the political and cultural schism between the plains and the tribal areas and the tribes themselves, of which there is still evidence today. One important reason for the current spread of rebellion in the region, is the random demarcation of the tribals' land to satisfy the interests of colonizers and the arbitrary isolation of the people. Unfortunately, this region is now politically in the grasp of different forms of government, that is, officially the region falls under the Indian Democratic Government but almost all the States are under the dominance of the self-professed underground government that consists of a number of insurgent factions. These insurgency outfits not only fight against the Indian Government but also fight with each other for their own personal interest and the quest for power. The people are forced to adhere to the Indian government as well as the self-professed government, struggling under the tyranny of many governing bodies.[11]

Amid terror, instability, militarization, economic neglect, migration, and experiences of racism in the region, Angami retrieves the "liberating elements" of her tradition's spirituality "for the construction of a postcolonial tribal feminist theology."[12]

I turn to Angami in this comparative essay because, as a scholar of Hindu-Christian relations, I am interested in how questions of indigeneity and land play out in the Indian context, where comparative work has tended to focus on India's dominant textual and ritual traditions. I also appreciate how she contributes to the ongoing project of feminist God-talk, which is a vocation that she and I share. In Angami's context, an earlier generation of tribal Christian theologians joined other Indigenous theologians from around the world in cultural and theological criticism of spirit-matter dualisms of Western Christian theology. Observing the remnants of androcentric and anthropocentric hierarchies in these Indigenous theologies, she applies a postcolonial feminist lens to deepen their emphasis on divine immanence.[13] She draws on Naga categories to recognize that "each creature is . . . endowed with a particular spirit and they all complement each other in vitalizing life." [14] I incorporate Angami's tribal Christian perspective into this comparative conversation in order to illuminate possible answers to the questions Dumont raises for me about the agency and teachings of the land in my local context.

Choosing these comparands requires resisting the customary, essentialized, dominant definitions of traditions. Tiemeier points to An Yountae's emphasis on the creolization of religion—in other words, on the fact that religious traditions of colonized and enslaved peoples combine elements to create community and solidarity. Lived Indigenous worldviews belong to the subject matter of comparative theology no less than the so-called "world religions" (which were never as uniform as the textbooks would have us believe). Creolized religious forms overstep the boundaries created by those with the power to define right belief and practice and to draw firm lines between self and other. Creolization is inherently "comparative and multireligious"; therefore, comparative theologians can and must treat religious and spiritual traditions in their hybridity, mixture, and complexity. Doing so is a step toward a decolonized theological practice.[15]

ALF DUMONT
My initial encounter with Alf Dumont's thought was through a text: he published his memoir when I was Principal of Emmanuel College, and I was privileged to attend a reading from the book that the College hosted on Zoom in November 2020. My next encounter with his thought came in the form of a coyote. I was reading his book while I was on retreat at Five Oaks Education and Retreat Centre, which is located at the confluence of two rivers on land that has long been sacred to local Indigenous people. I took my current spiritual struggles and my reflections on Dumont's book on a winter hike. Ruminating on recent changes in my life, I began to spiral into regret and self-pity; and just then, a coyote crossed my path. I had to laugh—the divine trickster was making an appearance, sending me the message that I should take my life less seriously. I would not have been attuned to this presence if it were not for the gift of Dumont's book.[16]

Dumont does not directly outline a theology of the land in his memoir. Rather, the land's agency appears in narrative form. In a chapter titled "Lessons by the River," he writes,

> Some of the most powerful teachings that come to us come when we least expect them and sometimes when we least want them. I have had teachings come to me this way. All of us have. Sometimes we are given the teachings, and we welcome them. Sometimes we walk away, turn our backs on the teachings, until the Holy, the Spirit, brings those teachings again later in life. Or *Gekek* [Hawk] or *Migizi* [Eagle] calls out

to us from afar to watch what path we are going down, for what looks like fun and adventure might not be. Or *Migizi* cries out from above to '*Wassa inaabidaa!*' (look in all directions). Perhaps that turn in the road, that twist in the river, may call up a teaching or an experience that cannot be avoided.[17]

For example, Dumont narrates encounters with *Makwa* (Bear) across the trajectory of his life, both on the land and in dreams. Experiences with bears frame the story of his brother's drowning in the river, which Dumont witnessed at the age of 11. *Makwa*, known as a healer, is integral to his healing from fear, guilt, and grief. Dumont also names "*Wiisagi ma'iingan* (coyote), *Aandeg* (crow) . . . *Waynaboozhoo* (spirit in Ojibwe; also known as *Nanibojou*), the laughing Jesus, and the Holy," as among the "spirit guides," with whom he is in regular conversation.[18]

What is the theological status of these spirits? Dumont is aware that naming this joyful plurality could be taken as "disrespect" and clarifies that he refers to them "out of a profound respect for their presence in my life and how their presence helps me to experience the Creator's presence or, to say it in another way, God's presence."[19] Using Christian terminology, he relates these spiritual presences to his experience of being "guided by 'the Spirit,'" his "sense [of] the holy other around me all the time," and "experiences that I can only explain as deeply spiritual and that involve the presence of the Spirit."[20] He invokes negative theology to root these expressions in the divine mystery and the inadequacy of human language.

Dumont concludes the memoir with a question-and-answer section, in which he addresses the theological questions he often receives by drawing upon these themes:

Do You Believe in the Trinity?
If by the Trinity—God's presence expressed in different ways—you mean respect for other people's belief, a willingness to walk with others in their understanding of the world, . . . then yes, I believe . . .
Do You Believe in God?
If by God, you mean the nameless mystery that we with our limited imaginations and words refer to as *Gitche Manido* (Great Spirit), *Kadabendgi* (Creator), *YHWH* (I am that I am), *Elohim* (God or gods), *Para Brahma* (Absolute Truth), *Adi Purush* (Timeless Being), Shiva (Benefactor), Nirankar (Formless One), Allah (The God), Bahá (All

Glorious), *Wankan Tanka* (Great Spirit), or *Ahura Mazda* (Lord Wisdom), then yes, I believe.

The book's subtitle, "From Church Pew to Sweat Lodge," signals Dumont's journey to reach these affirmations of plurality. He and his brother, Jim Dumont, took different spiritual paths: Jim as a traditional Anishinaabe elder, Alf as a United Church minister. "My brother and I agreed to honor each other's way of walking in the world and to respect the deep teachings of both spiritualities," he writes. *How* he would do this was unclear to him at the time.[21] He had a vision of himself "being sandwiched between two other parts of me, like three bodies, one on top of the other."[22] He felt pressure from both sides of his identity. First Nations cultural values made demands of him from one side. Christian condemnations of Indigenous ways wrestled with loving and accepting interpretations of Christian teachings on the other.

Dumont writes of a sweat lodge ceremony undertaken while teaching a group of students from Emmanuel College. He was compelled to stay longer than usual in the lodge, where he overheard a conversation with Jesus and *Waynaboozhoo*. Each affirmed the difficulty of living up to the wise teachings of their traditions. Each affirmed the importance of laughter. Then they agreed, "We do not need to walk the journey alone. We can walk with each other respectfully, without saying that ours is the only true way."[23] Humility and courage would be essential to the walking.

Humor is also key to Dumont's approach, which is also rooted in the teachings of the natural world. Beyond the Christian themes of God's transcendence and the Holy Spirit's presence, he connects the Indigenous notion of the trickster to the Holy Spirit's activity in his life. Holding language loosely, he professes that "God has a great sense of humor and is a God of love, not a God of vengeance or judgment" in relation to changing human apprehensions of the divine.[24] *Wiisagi ma'iingan* (coyote) is a recurring character in his life story, showing up at many junctions where life takes an unexpected turn, or where a settled truth gets upended. This playful attitude helps him to acknowledge that the answers he has reached are *his* answers, that he has "made peace" with the traditional and Christian ways, and that "my way of looking at life is not your way of looking at life."[25]

When I had the opportunity to ask Dumont about the spirits and their relation to the divine, he pointed me to Jesus' prayer to God "that they may all be one, as you . . . are in me and I am in you" (John 17:21). Mysteriously, the "spiritual guides" are "in" God, as Jesus and his followers are in God. As Jesus is "one" with God and prays the same for all beings, the spirits of the land are one with God. Thus, Dumont writes of Jesus as someone who taught others "to embrace both our humanness and our divinity, our spirituality, as Jesus did, [and] become one with God as Jesus was."[26]

> Those spiritual guides *Waynaboozhoo, Wiisagi ma'iingan, Weesekayjack, Aandeg, Makwa, Migizi, Gekek,* the Holy, and Jesus . . . call out to us, and call out something from us, something from deep inside. The land does that, too. The land shares her story and sings her song. The land with the heartbeat of mother earth, known through the sound of the drum, and our heartbeats as human beings are so very close.[27]

The above passage is one of the few in which Dumont explicitly names the land as one of the spirits. All of the spirits, including that of the land herself, are one. Our responsibility is to live in good relation with them.[28]

Before shifting to the other comparand in this study, let us review: Dumont writes about land as a category relatively infrequently. He most often teaches asymptotically through narrative and humor, with a strong emphasis on the individual's learning through experience. These two features prove to be related when Dumont relates his experience in a non-prescriptive manner that allows each person to listen to the land for themselves: "I do not ask anyone to follow my theology or my spirituality. I ask, instead, that people develop their own theological or spiritual directions based on individual spiritual experiences and individual understandings of the truth. I was taught to listen to the drumbeat, and the heartbeat of your mother, the heartbeat of mother earth, and go in the direction the heart is leading."[29] Nevertheless, as is the case for fellow Anishinaabe theorist John Borrows, whom I cited in the introduction to this paper, "the land" in this context refers inclusively to many natural, animal, elemental, and geographical phenomena. Therefore, Dumont's robust engagement with the animal characters populating the land and the spiritual world, and his direct theologizing of these characters as "spiritual guides," can be taken as a basis for understanding his theology of land as enspirited—that is, full of presences and guides that are one with the divine.

KENEIPFENUO RÜPREO ANGAMI

We look now to a second Indigenous Christian context, the Northeast of India, where Keneipfenuo Rüpreo Angami considers the theological status of the spirits operative in the land. In contrast to Dumont's genres of memoir and non-prescriptive testimony, Angami works out the spiritual and theological implications of listening to the aliveness of the earth through her Ph.D. dissertation at the Radboud University, Nijmegen. I do not turn to her work to impose another theological interpretation upon Dumont's experiences or to say that her thesis is what he intends. Rather, with my interest piqued by his brief and allusive claim about the relation of the land to the divine, I want to ask: what can I, as a white settler theologian, learn in the space between the two thinkers about the spirit and agency of the land where I live and work?

Angami draws upon theological concepts from the dialect of the Tenyimia ethnic group, which includes "seven tribes: the Angami, Chakhesang, Mao, Poumai, Puchury, Rengma and Zeliang, living across three states: Assam, Manipur and Nagaland."[30] Her postcolonial strategy retrieves suppressed histories, oral traditions, and tribal women's resistance to colonial representation "for emancipating the faith and the life of the tribals."[31] Angami describes the primal religion of the tribes before colonization thus:

> They worshiped benevolent spirits and nature such as river, trees, sun, moon, et cetera. Some tribes worshiped their ancestors as well. Even though Primal religion did not have any sacred written scripture like other religions, . . . religion permeates all facets of life and determines the overall life activities of the people . . . There exists a cosmic sense of oneness as there is no clear-cut distinction between the sacred and the secular, between religious and non-religious, nor between the spiritual and material aspects of life.[32]

Within this holistic worldview, all things relate to the land, which "as a whole was considered to be sacred because it is believed to be the dwelling place of the Divine."[33] This belief entails being "a good steward by taking care of nature" and practicing life cycle rites and annual festivals that recognize the "affinity between the different forms of divinity, humans and other creations."[34]

The colonial missionaries taught that Christianity held exclusive access to truth, that tribal religion was superstitious and backward, and that "the material world [was] of little importance and even evil."³⁵ The missionaries forbade tribal rites, worship, and observance of taboos. Angami describes how, "as a consequence, the Primal religious belief in the Divine as animated in creation, was replaced by the transcendent God who is not a part of the physical world."³⁶ This theology drastically changed the worldview of the converts, whose outlook became increasingly anthropocentric rather than rooted in relationship to the land. Western missionaries rejected feminine and mother images for the creator in favor of patriarchal names. They introduced a hierarchical structure in which a high divinity rules over the world. They translated imperial God-language (Almighty, King, Lord) into local terms that persist in the tribal Christian imagination. Their emphasis on classical monotheism "not only led to the total rejection of other notions of religion but also completely negated the multiplicity of Divinity that was very much ingrained in the tribal Primal religious world."³⁷

Angami's analysis joins other tribal theologians in retrieving the Naga people's traditional lack of "dichotomy or dualism . . . between body and spirit, the spiritual and the material," which "made the adherents of Primal religion [be] more sensitive to their co-creatures."³⁸ She builds upon the work of Wati Longchar, a prominent tribal (Ao Naga) theologian of the elder generation who emphasizes the immanence of the divine in his treatment of the land. His theology makes important ecological interventions, and it denounces the economic and political structures that have made Indigenous populations vulnerable to displacement and state violence.

With Longchar, Angami defines land expansively to include animals and other beings: "Land brings together Supreme Being, spirits, ancestors and creation as one family, because for Longchar, without the land it is impossible for people to co-exist with other living beings, their ancestors and God."³⁹ Longchar's theology is distinctly space centered. He contrasts the colonial view of land as "'wilderness' or 'empty space,'" with the Naga view, in which "the land is our temple (cathedral), our university, our hospitality, our sustenance, the vast hall where we congregate and celebrate our parent, our life."⁴⁰ Land is so central to Naga identity and spirituality that to lose their traditional territory threatens their very existence. Divinity and land are similarly inseparable: "For example, the Aos and Sangtams of Nagaland (India) call their Supreme Being, *Lijaba*. *Li* means 'land' and *jaba* means 'real.' It means the Supreme Being is 'the real soil.' Sometimes people call the Supreme Being, *Lizaba*. *Li* means 'soil' and *zaba* means 'enter,' meaning 'the one who enters or indwells into the soil.'"[41] In this context, communities observe taboos in order to exercise restraint in harvesting certain animals and foods; and they honor totems to denote a special relationship between a plant or animal and the community which protects and lives in symbiosis with it.[42]

Angami wants deeper attention to gender in this analysis. Ecological devastation is related to the devaluation of tribal women and women's bodies that ensued when the missionaries introduced the transcendent, androcentric God and banished the feminine divine.[43] Though Longchar critiques the model of the transcendent, impassive Father God who resides in heaven, Angami wonders why he chooses to import classical Western philosophical terminology to defend tribal ways of being against the charge of pantheism.[44] She writes, "Regrettably, the kyriarchal nature of androcentric classical language has crept into tribal theology, and tribal theology was not all-inclusive. Longchar, for example, has comprehensively articulated his tribal theology, centered on the concept of 'Land' or 'Space,' but for tribal women it is difficult to relate to this theology because of its androcentric theological articulations and because most of the tribal wo/men never enjoyed landownership, so that 'Land Theology' situates wo/men on the margins."[45] From her feminist perspective, land's centrality carries ambivalence. Although land is constitutive of tribal identity, inheritance traditionally passed from fathers to sons, and "even in a matrilineal society, women did not have any say in relation to land as the maternal uncle made all the decisions regarding the land."[46]

Beyond centering the land, Angami wants to dig more deeply to retrieve tribal theological principles that subvert patriarchal and colonial hegemonies. Longchar emphasizes transcendent and immanent divinity in Primal traditions. However, Angami observes that by using this Western philosophical binary (transcendent-immanent), he reinscribes it and attributes classical Greek attributes to divine transcendence. In addition, she finds him overly concerned with defending his view against the Western phobia toward pantheism when he insists that "the Divine manifests him/herself in natural objects and phenomena and is both outside and beyond creation."[47] Kyriarchal notions also linger in other liberation theologies of Northeast India in hierarchical, imperial language like "Supreme Being" and "Wholly Other."[48]

Angami aims to define the theological status of the spirits in her community's traditional worldview without resorting to classical theism, explaining that, before the Christian missionaries arrived, "tribals were worshiping a number of spirits."[49] She does not distinguish between worship and adoration, as Christians have sometimes done in response to iconoclasm but observes, "Natural objects and creations were accepted as symbols of the presence of the Divine, and adoration and oblations [were] performed from time to time . . . Divinity is immanent in nature, an integral part of creation."[50] She subverts the binaries of immanent-transcendent or high and low gods by staying close to the ontological categories of the Krüna (meaning "ancestors' belief") traditions of the Angami tribe. For example, the first category of divine being is the source of all creation (what Angami terms "the Divine"), called *Terhuomia* and *Ukepenuopfü* interchangeably. *Terhuomia*, designating the divine protector and provider, is flexible in terms of number, and it is non-anthropomorphic and gender-neutral. The missionaries co-opted this term to denote Satan and evil spirits. *Ukepenuopfü*, "she who births us," is feminine and maternal. The missionaries retained the term but used it to describe the patriarchal Father God they preached.[51] The second category of beings to be worshipped are "the different kinds of benevolent spirits, malevolent spirits and spirits of the ancestors," which assist or impede daily agrarian life and receive the people's "reverence, appreciation, and thanksgiving."[52] These invisible and mysterious spirits "signify the intrinsic relationship between the creator and the creatures and amongst the creatures," endow each creature with worth, empower them, and put them in essential relation with one another.[53] The missionaries dismissed these spirits as superstition or demonic.

The category of *Ruopfü* (Spirit) encompasses both of these categories by referring to "all supernatural entities to whom tribals dedicated rituals, worshiped and prayed."[54]

> Tribals focused profoundly on the worship of spirits. In the *Tenyidie* dialect, *Ruopfü* (Spirit) had a very important place in Primal religion, in fact the whole of creation was considered to be animated with *Ruopfü*, which had a feminine connotation [grammatical ending, *pfü*]. The belief that spirits animate all creatures, formed the essence of tribal people's religious beliefs. Certain elements, rocks, trees, lakes, rivers, or a particular place were revered because they were believed to be animated with *Ruopfü*. These spirits could be either benevolent or malevolent and of either sex. The benevolent spirits were felt to be responsible for the prosperity and welfare of the villages, while

the malevolent spirits were considered to be destructive and causing suffering, sickness, accidents, sudden death and mental illness. The benevolent spirits guarded the community or village from diseases, epidemics, pestilence and natural calamities and devastations, such as crop failure, storms, and floods.[55]

Ruopfü defies categories such as transcendence and immanence. In chorus with other feminist and postcolonial theologians, Angami reminds readers that the Divine is beyond language (*via negativa*), calls for many names (*via analogica*), and exceeds categories (*via eminentia*). The excess of the divine calls for recognition of divine presence in human and non-human life, the natural world, and the cosmos.

Angami's term for God's envelopment of "the great organism of which we are all part" is the Copious Divine.[56] She follows Elisabeth Schüssler Fiorenza's treatment of the *via eminentia* in relation to feminist retrieval of Goddesses: "such re-mythologization does not result in polytheism as long as it is not constructed in ontological terms and remains within the rhetorical boundaries of the *via negativa* and the *via analogica*."[57] Laurel Schneider's theology of multiplicity, which was developed in conversation with Native American traditions, further assists Angami in challenging classical monotheism's "logic of the One": "The concept of multiplicity—*multus*—which does not mean numerous but signifies that there is more, opens up monotheism to a comprehensive and broad articulation of the Divine."[58] Oneness is included as an expression of multiplicity in which different elements constitute one another. When Angami theologizes the many spirits of Primal religious traditions as *Ruopfü*, this multiplicity "does not posit that each spirit is the intrinsic essence of the Divine," but rather manifests divinity, showing "that the Divine is not a totally transcendent Divine but that there is a touch of the Divine in the creation."[59]

A PLACE FOR SPIRITS IN THEOLOGY

As we set out to compare these works by Dumont and Angami, we must again be clear about what we are *not* doing. We are not seeking to extract a decontextualized "Indigenous wisdom." Each of their worldviews has its own integrity. Neither would impose their interpretations upon the other or upon us as readers. The works have different audiences. Dumont frames his work explicitly with reference to the United Church of Canada and uses anecdotes about the people and churches that are important to his story. He narrates his experiences in a manner accessible to laypeople. He emphasizes that the book is *his* story, that the theological concepts he articulates are *his* truths, and that each person must be on their own spiritual path to listen to the heartbeat within the land and discover what is true. Writing for an international scholarly audience, Angami has different goals. She explicates the history and theory that undergirds her constructive theology. She aims to empower tribal Christians to claim their own cultural heritage theologically, equip non-tribal theologians to understand the implications of feminist and postcolonial theologies for her context, and contribute to the decolonization of the discipline more broadly.

When we place the two theologians side-by-side and allow their projects to shine upon one another, it is clear that they share the decolonial priority of self-definition. In contrast to the missionaries who introduced Christianity to their communities generations ago, they view their ancestral traditions positively and draw upon the categories and stories of those traditions to craft their own theological outlooks. Longchar has described this as the "self-theologizing" stage of Indigenous theologies, in which "Indigenous people themselves must do their own theology relevant to their context . . . [and] take the healing of Indigenous communities into their own hand."[60] Self-definition through traditional wisdom and practices draws both theologians to the aliveness of the land and the multiplicity of spirits therein. They both acknowledge the friction that experiences with these beings create for the dominant Christian theologies in their contexts; yet both choose to honor the importance of traditional stories, practices, and relationships with animals and the land.

The theological scope, doctrinal foci, and communities of accountability of the two proposals differ. While Angami develops the doctrine of God, Dumont often reflects on the spirits in the context of Christology. Angami's work focuses on the nature of God as incomprehensible and excessive divinity. Drawing upon feminist and postcolonial theologians, her constructive proposal is bold and has far-reaching consequences for reconstructing the orthodoxy of western Christian thought. She stretches the bounds of monotheism by taking seriously her community's experiences of the multiplicity of the spirits of the land. Dumont's theological offerings are humbler in scope as he charts a path between the two traditions in his heritage. Like Angami, Dumont appeals to the undefinable nature of the Holy. However, given his accountability to the church, Jesus's teaching provides the template as he emphasizes the oneness rather than the multiplicity of spirit: we are all spirit, and we are all related and interconnected in the great mystery of life.

Each project has different implications for spiritual practice and understanding. Angami's emphasis on divine multiplicity begins from the everyday worship of Naga people. People experience *Ruopfü* as both unified and multiple in their day-to-day lives. In this ontology, Spirit(s) animate and give energy to created beings, living and nonliving. Though she recognizes resemblances with the Christian concept of the Holy Spirit (*ruach*, *pneuma*, wind, energy, source of life), *Ruopfü* is "a broader metaphor in re-imagining the Divine," encompassing the source of all life as well as the many spirits that inhabit the world and receive worship.[61] For his part, Dumont prefers not to use the language of worship for the human relation to the spirits: we may walk with them and talk to them; we must take only what we need and give them thanks.[62] He observes that "Jesus never said to worship him. He always pointed back to the one he came from."[63] Jesus is, therefore, among numerous "spirit guides" Dumont has met. Although he has not met them "as I have met people in my life," he writes, "I carry on regular dialogues with all of them. Sometimes they come to me through the wisdom and the care offered by others. Sometimes they come as a spiritual presence that I cannot explain to others."[64]

What is a settler theologian like me to do with these rich and distinct theological visions? Borrows likens the process of encountering Indigenous methodologies to "a few grains of yeast in the preparation of bread" that can "positively lift the entire institution."[65] Thus, as a settler living on Anishinaabe territory, when I read across these two different contexts and modes of theological reflection, I begin to expand my scholarly and theological "repertoire."[66] The tasks of decolonization are not only for the colonized. For people from hegemonic Western contexts, Angami encourages "the deconstruction of one's own imperialistic thinking and the identification of the multiple layers that confront life."[67] Learning from Indigenous theologies may be the only way to properly revise ingrained Western (Christian) dualisms between spirit and matter and to become open to the powers these dualisms obscure.

Learning about local Indigenous ontologies should challenge how non-Indigenous theologians think about the land. In Dumont's memoir, I encounter some of the spirits of the place where I live. In Angami, I see one way to build out the theological conditions for understanding the wisdom of the land. The hard boundaries of monotheism soften beyond trinitarian multiplicity. Customary categories of the Supreme Being's paradoxical transcendence and immanence dissolve into a copious concept of the divine. These ideas reverberate cross-culturally and echo across other global and historical contexts, in which Western hierarchies and definitions do not set the terms of discourse.[68]

SOLIDARITY AND THE LAND

Comparative theologians have been urged to go beyond the rectification of theological frameworks and enter political solidarity with the people of the land. In Tiemeier's vision, comparative theology must "align with the comparative cosmopolitical theology of colonized, creolized peoples, and commit to new ways of being in the world that prioritize relational solidarity and justice."[69] Those who attend to a world where lived traditions have been forged in the conditions of colonization will expect and embrace their hybrid nature. Furthermore, Tiemeier challenges white comparative theologians to focus on lived religion rather than texts and abstractions and to work in full and accountable relationship with the communities we write about.[70] Although my learning from the Indigenous nations where I live and study is still in an early phase and does not meet this high bar, as a provisional step in this direction, we can listen to what Angami and Dumont are (and are not) saying about the politics of the land.

There are many ways to relate to the land. Settlers are guests on the traditional (and often unceded) territories of Indigenous people. One implication of this acknowledgment is that settler governments should give the land back to those communities or govern the territories jointly as equal and autonomous nations. Another is that individual settlers can pay reparations, such as a portion of their rent, to local Indigenous communities in recognition of and gratitude for living and working there.[71] These may be good paths forward, and land justice movements are part of both the Canadian and Indian contexts; yet neither of the two theologians discussed here emphasizes land as territory to be claimed, returned, or governed. Why?

Dumont acknowledges that First Nations sometimes must use the language of land ownership for political purposes when dealing with political parties and corporations. Indigenous communities have also fought one another to control territory. However, he counsels that it is better to step back from the temptation to grasp at power and to walk humbly. In his Ojibwe worldview, "no one owns the land." Having been placed on the land, humans were given responsibility for certain parts of it. All nations have the responsibility to protect the forests and the waters, to protest their destruction, and to share their wisdom. If we do not, "we will all be put in jeopardy." Relating to the land does not mean owning it; it means walking in a good and humble way with the land and all the people on the land.[72]

For Angami's part, although the Naga people have been witnesses to multiple, overlapping waves of colonization and ongoing chaos, she does not side with the insurgent tribal groups who demand autonomy over territory. She observes that land ownership and governance have never fallen to women, whether in traditional models or under other governments. Furthermore, the insurgents contribute to the terror that envelops ordinary existence in her community. (She wrote the introduction to her dissertation in Nagaland to the sound of gunfire and teargas dispersing an angry crowd protesting a policy of the Indian government.[73]) Instead, Angami retrieves tribal women's non-violent movements that "focus on practical, social, and political issues that affect women, for instance . . . rape, sexual molestation, murder, militarization, and social menaces such as alcohol, drugs, HIV/AIDS."[74] She puts the community's holistic well-being ahead of desires to dominate the land and political rivals.[75]

The theological perspectives encountered here invite deep attentiveness to the Spirit's multiple manifestations in the livingness of creation. Listening closely to the land, we may hear the divine speaking in many voices—human and non-human, personal and non-personal. The perspectives and priorities of these whispering spirits decenter our own. Dominant Christian theologies strain to accommodate these realities. The hybrid (or creolized) perspectives of Indigenous Christian theologians such as Dumont and Angami must become part of the theological repertoire if imperial theology is ever to lose its grip on Christianity's relation to the land.

NOTES

1. "Sandy-Saulteaux Spiritual Centre." For a powerful demonstration of the land's pedagogy from an Anishinaabe perspective, see Simpson, *As We Have Always Done*.
2. Borrows, *Law's Indigenous Ethics*, 160.
3. Watts, "Indigenous Place-thought & Agency," 31.
4. I'm grateful to my colleague, Jonathan Hamilton-Diabo, for elucidating these tensions for me. Personal conversation, June 21, 2022.

5. Tiemeier, "Decolonization," 90. Cf. Joshi, *White Christian Privilege*.
6. TRC, *Calls to Action*, 1.
7. Borrows, *Law's Indigenous Ethics*, 160.
8. Dumont, *The Other Side*, viii.
9. Dumont, *The Other Side*, 135.
10. Angami, *Copious*, 12-14.
11. Angami, *Copious*, 37.
12. Angami, *Copious*, 43.
13. Angami, *Copious*, 2-4.
14. Angami, *Copious*, 223.
15. Tiemeier, "Decolonization," 88.
16. I immediately recalled a lecture by Laurel Schneider, in which she challenges comparative theologians to expand beyond text-based methods. See Schneider, "When the Book is a Coyote."
17. Dumont, *The Other Side*, 59.
18. Dumont, *The Other Side*, xiv.
19. Dumont, *The Other Side*, xv.
20. Dumont, *The Other Side*, xv.
21. Dumont, *The Other Side*, 29. The brothers converse about their different paths in *Dumont Brothers: The Paths of the Spirit*.
22. Dumont, *The Other Side*, 30.
23. Dumont, *The Other Side*, 13.
24. Dumont, *The Other Side*, xv.
25. Dumont, *The Other Side*, vii, 177.
26. Dumont, *The Other Side*, 11.
27. Dumont, *The Other Side*, 17.
28. Alf Dumont, personal conversation, June 23, 2022.
29. Dumont, *The Other Side*, viii.
30. Angami, *Copious*, 93n316.
31. Angami, *Copious*, 67.
32. Angami, *Copious*, 15, cf. 98.
33. Angami, *Copious*, 98.
34. Angami, *Copious*, 98
35. Angami, *Copious*, 124
36. Angami, *Copious*, 117.
37. Angami, *Copious*, 207.
38. Angami, *Copious*, 123.
39. Angami, *Copious*, 210n746.
40. Longchar, *Returning to Mother Earth*, 28.
41. Longchar, *Returning to Mother Earth*, 28-29.
42. Longchar, *Returning to Mother Earth*, 39.
43. Angami, *Copious*, 124-29.
44. Angami, *Copious*, 208-209.

45. Angami, *Copious*, 210–11. In her usage, the term "wo/men" denotes women and colonized men who experience the underside of imperial power. She follows Elisabeth Schüsler Fiorenza in using the term "kyriarchy" to denote not only gender hierarchy ("patriarchy") but also entire systems that subject certain classes of people to the "lordship" (*kyrios*, "Lord") of others.
46. Angami, *Copious*, 95. Inatoli Aye further queers Angami's gender critique by noting Longchar's tendency to portray divinity in heteronormative, phallic terms in relation to the Earth (Aye, "Queer(y)ing," 47).
47. Angami, *Copious*, 209
48. Angami, *Copious*, 211. The Western missionaries introduced the "classical God" to converts using male names "such as *Puo* (One), *Puou* (Father), *Nuou* (Son), *Kediu* (King), *Niepuu* (Lord), *Kekuotho-u* (Almighty one), *Teigeikebau* (One in the heavens)" (Angami, *Copious*, 212).
49. Angami, *Copious*, 210.
50. Angami, *Copious*, 98–99.
51. Angami, *Copious*, 211–16.
52. Angami, *Copious*, 217.
53. Angami, *Copious*, 219.
54. Angami, *Copious*, 217.
55. Angami, *Copious*, 101–102.
56. Angami, *Copious*, 222.
57. Angami, *Copious*, 200.
58. Angami, *Copious*, 203.
59. Angami, *Copious*, 224.
60. Longchar, *Returning to Mother Earth*, 81.
61. Angami, *Copious*, 221.
62. Dumont, personal conversation, June 23, 2022.
63. *Dumont Brothers*, 11:25.
64. Dumont, *The Other Side*, xv.
65. Borrows, *Law's Indigenous Ethics*, 160.
66. Borrows, *Law's Indigenous Ethics*, 160.
67. Angami, *Copious*, 50.
68. Further work on the multiplicity of spirits and powers in the Christian theological inheritance would consider scholarship on early Christianity such as Fredricksen, *Paul*; biblical and theological principles such as *dunamis* and *energeia* such as Barnes, *The Power of God*; contemporary lived religion such as Orsi, *History and Presence*; and cross-cultural Christian theological scholarship such as Schneider, *Beyond Monotheism*.
69. Tiemeier, "Decolonization," 89. She continues, "White Christian comparative theologians and the Western academy . . . must be proactive and brutally self-critical. They must be honest about their power, privilege, and contexts. They must center voices other than their own and be in relational solidarity" (Tiemeier, "Decolonization," 91).

70. Tiemeier, "Decolonization," 90–91.
71. For perspectives on "how to return land in so-called Canada to Indigenous peoples," see *Briarpatch*, "The Land Back Issue."
72. Dumont, personal conversation, June 23, 2022.
73. Angami, *Copious*, 1.
74. Angami, *Copious*, 140–41.
75. Similarly focused recommendations exist for the nation of Canada. See National Inquiry, *Reclaiming Power and Place*.

REFERENCES

Angami, Keneipfenuo Rüpreo. *Copious Amidst Chaos: A Tribal Postcolonial Feminist God-Talk from Northeast Indian Perspective*. Nijmegen: Ipskamp Printing Nijmegen, 2018.

Aye, Inatoli. "Queer(y)ing Naga Indigenous Theology." *Feminist Theology* 30, no. 1 (2021): 37–51. https://doi.org/10.1177/09667350211031181.

Barnes, Michel René. *The Power of God: Dunamis in Gregory of Nyssa's Trinitarian Theology*. Washington, DC: The Catholic University of America Press, 1999.

Briarpatch. "The Land Back Issue." *Briarpatch* (Sept.–Oct. 2020). https://briarpatchmagazine.com/issues/view/september-october-2020.

Borrows, John. *Law's Indigenous Ethics*. Toronto: University of Toronto Press, 2019.

Dumont, Alf. *The Other Side of the River: From Church Pew to Sweat Lodge*. Toronto: United Church Publishing House, 2020.

Fredricksen, Paula. *Paul: The Pagans' Apostle*. New Haven, CT: Yale University Press, 2017.

Joshi, Khyati Y. *White Christian Privilege: The Illusion of Religious Equality in America*. New York: New York University Press, 2020.

Longchar, A. Wati. *Returning to Mother Earth: Theology, Christian Witness and Theological Education, An Indigenous Perspective*. Kolkata: PTCA/SCEPTRE, 2012.

National Inquiry into Missing and Murdered Indigenous Women and Girls. *Reclaiming Power and Place: The Final Report of the National Inquiry into Missing and Murdered Indigenous Women and Girls*. Vancouver: Privy Council Office, 2019. https://www.mmiwg-ffada.ca/final-report/

Orsi, Robert. *History and Presence*. Cambridge, MA: Harvard University Press, 2016.

"Sandy-Saulteaux Spiritual Centre." Sandy-Saulteaux. Accessed January 24, 2023. https://sandysaulteaux.ca/.

Schneider, Laurel. "When the Book is a Coyote: Some Challenges and Possibilities for Comparative Theology from Native American Traditions." Harvard Center for the Study of World Religions. April 7, 2015. https://news-archive.hds.harvard.edu/news/2015/04/07/video-when-book-coyote

———. *Beyond Monotheism: A Theology of Multiplicity*. New York: Routledge, 2008.

Simpson, Leanne Betasamosake. *As We Have Always Done: Indigenous Freedom through Radical Resistance*. Minneapolis: University of Minnesota Press, 2020.

Tiemeier, Tracy Sayuki. "White Christian Privilege and the Decolonization of Comparative Theology." In *The Human in a Dehumanizing World: Reexamining Theological Anthropology and Its Implications*, edited by Jessica Coblentz and Daniel P. Horan, 85–95. Maryknoll, NY: Orbis Books, 2022.

Tindal, Mardi, prod. *Dumont Brothers: The Paths of the Spirit*. Toronto: Berkeley Studios/United Church of Canada, 1992. Video.

Truth and Reconciliation Commission of Canada [TRC]. *Calls to Action*. Winnipeg: Truth and Reconciliation Commission of Canada, 2015. https://www2.gov.bc.ca/assets/gov/british-columbians-our-governments/Indigenous-people/aboriginal-peoples-documents/calls_to_action_english2.pdf

Watts, Vanessa. "Indigenous Place-thought & Agency Amongst Humans and Non-humans (First Woman and Sky Woman Go on a European World Tour!)." *Decolonization: Indigeneity, Education & Society* 2, no. 1 (2013): 20–34.

DOMENIK ACKERMANN

CONCLUSION

The most recent generation of scholars engaging in comparative theological discourse has elevated issues of decoloniality and questions around decentering Western Christian theology. The discourses in this issue of *CrossCurrents* strive to be in line with a decolonial approach both on a meta-level and on the level of theological content. Indeed, in all of the articles presented here, the contributors imply that a comparative theology that wishes to engage seriously in decoloniality must reflect on and rethink the meaning of land, with its many facets of meaning and importance. On the topic, the contributions to this special issue on theologies of land not only showcase a kaleidoscope of meanings that land can have but also reveal that there is potential for further comparative theological engagement. We delineated how places, soil, and geography have theological meanings that reach into relevant meta-theological questions, as well as cultural and even political conversations.

By way of conclusion, I should like only to mention possible pathways for further conversation. Clearly, the relevance of land with respect to religious traditions' identities reaches beyond the four perspectives presented here. There has been engagement in historical theology and the question of colonization, as well as studies in scriptures about the meaning of land, soil, and Israel. However, discourse across and between traditions is still a novelty. Our discourse on land, specifically, provokes me to think about what perspectives present themselves from native traditions outside the Batak, Anishinaabe, or Naga traditions. What further insights about the significance of land can we gain from the ongoing cultural-political discourses with Native people in colonized countries (such as those in North America, Africa, and Australia, to name just a few)? How can dialogue about land include Muslim insights, especially in the context of conversations about Israel and Palestine? These are but a few questions of many that must be asked. Finally, how can land, as a paradox between porosity and particularity, help us further understand multiplicity and interconnectedness?

The conversations that the four of us engaged in during the process of compiling this issue were rich and insightful. It is our hope that this conversation sparks interest in a broader theological conversation. I personally thank Michelle Voss Roberts, Hesron Sihombing and O'neil van Horn for availing themselves and creating these thoughtful and thought-provoking articles. I also thank Paul Hedges for introducing us, and S. Brent Rodriguez-Plate for offering *CrossCurrents* as an outlet for our conversations.

SHANNON HARDWICK

FOR JANE, ON HER NEPHEW'S BIRTHDAY
—AFTER JANE COOPER

And your poems did allow for the unseen,
the unnoticed truth of others—uncovered
just so, just
                as the girl paused mid-thought, mid-bite, and yet,
who lent their ears to your secret, your triple-locked door,
your tunneling hour before
                        the room suddenly spilled white?

That the Winter Road led you to St. Malo,
and your father's parachute—
his blue on blue on blue,
how it rolled off your tongue like wind
before your journey was to begin.
For you, Jane—
a kaleidoscope of comfort, an eternal field of stars.
For your legacy—
it belongs to the unwanted, the unseen—humanity.
What you made of it—
your lifeblood, your little blue anchors of truth:
they survive in our future,
our long canyon, our echoing sea.

SHANNON HARDWICK

FOR JANE, THREE DAYS AFTER HER BROTHER'S PASSING
—AFTER JANE COOPER

Jane, your notebooks haunt us after the wake.
We stand up. We sit down. But the burn is slow
& you taught us grief can keep

long after letting-go. Oblivion starts to stir
in the first house built from a child's
scaffolding—your words & John's

laughter. We are left imagining
this autumn out of the pair of you, leaving
before us in early darkness. You attend to the space,

the radiance. *It's time to go*. But we call out, anyway,
into the air, like a body between us, but lighter.

REVIEWED BY AYA NIMER

LITTLE SYRIA, AT THE BROOKLYN ACADEMY OF MUSIC

Omar Offendum's musical show *Little Syria* nods to the rich history of Brooklyn's Syrian community and is part of a vibrant tradition of Syrian performances at the Brooklyn Academy of Music.[1] Offendum highlights this history by centering the rich visual language of *shammi* (Levantine) design, using mother-of-pearl chairs and gold decor to amplify the narrative style of the show and create a bridge between the audience and the historical titular neighborhood where the show is set. *Little Syria*, a collaboration with musicians Ronnie Malley, Thanks Joey, and Nano Raies, tells a story of Arabs in American life. By interweaving different narrative and musical techniques, Offendum shines a light on a historic Syrian neighborhood in Manhattan, New York and creates a space for communal healing.

Offendum uses multiple cultural touchstones to encapsulate the broader and more intimate histories of Little Syria, creating continuity in the historical narrative of Arabs in the United States. Offendum builds this historical narrative through two concurrent processes. The first is by telling the *broader* history of Little Syria and Arab immigration in tandem with the *intimate* histories of people in Little Syria. The second is the use of *hakawati*, an Arab storytelling tradition that relies on motifs such as allegory, music, and spectacle to tell a story. Offendum uses *hakawati* as a storytelling practice to interweave our own daily emotional experiences with those of Offendum's historical figures, giving us a parallax view of racism, finding a job, and making money.[2] The show begins with a track that outlines the experience of migrating to America through the lyrics "It's time for a new chapter / in this land of opportunity/ the promises of rapture and happily ever after/ lay behind these golden doors . . . allow me to explain before you butcher my name/ label me unhireable or worse yet undesirable / I'm a man with a heart and a soul on a mission / here to build a better life . . ." Starting the show with a broad picture of the

Figure 1. A snapshot of the stage and setup of Little Syria at the Brooklyn Academy of Music

anxieties and emotions associated with immigration creates an aperture for Offendum to take us into the lived experience of a street salesman in Little Syria.

The salesman sells his wares near an American soap factory that uses pig lard as a main ingredient. The owner of the factory often ridicules the Syrian salesman by calling him "dirty" and "unhygienic." The salesman thinks the ridicule is ironic considering Syrian soap's reputation as a valuable and potent cleansing agent. This segment animates the daily exchanges that comprised the lives of those living in Little Syria as they encountered racist institutions in their new neighborhood. This intimate history, which visualizes the emotional lives of historical figures, creates a space for us as viewers to reflect on our own experiences with racism. The interweaving of broad and intimate histories through *hakawati* shows how our emotional lives are intertwined with larger political histories.

The musical structure is similarly comprised of two elements interwoven into a distinct style. Thanks Joey began the process of creating the musical soundscape of the show by sampling Arabic songs from the mid-twentieth century, which were then overlaid with Offendum's lyrics and complemented by Ronnie Malley's oud performance. Offendum's

Figure 2. A backstage shot of Omar Offendum, Thanks Joey, and Ronnie Malley at the Brooklyn Academy of Music

lyrics, combined with Thanks Joey's beats, create a moment that fuses the historic Arab soundscape of the 1900s with Offendum's contemporary hip hop style. This is further developed in Ronnie's live oud performance. The oud is an instrument with strong cultural associations and memories for many Arab listeners. The nostalgic nature of the oud evokes a soundscape reminiscent of home, another way that *Little Syria* engages with intimate histories. This soundscape simultaneously feels historic and contemporary, transporting listeners into a liminal world that acknowledges and draws from both American and Arab culture.

Offendum's ability to create harmony and continuity through various cultural mediums and artistic structures within the show culminates in his performance of "Omarvelous," capturing a sense of coming to know one's self. The song seamlessly moves between Arabic and English as Offendum expresses his confidence in his artistic skills. Lyrics such as "Ya Allaaaaah!/ Nobody can upend him!/ Do I Offendum with my voice?/ Offendum with my lyrics? . . . Offendum with my eloquence?/ Offendum with my elegance?" demonstrate a self-definition that is continuous and dynamic. This confidence inspires within viewers a sense of enthusiasm and harmony for acknowledging and celebrating not only their history and culture, but also their own personal experiences. These experiences weave viewers into the tapestry Offendum has outlined in his performance—one of belonging, knowledge, and pride in our shared histories.

Little Syria maneuvers through a rich history and multiple artistic mediums to convey a message of cultural continuity and pride. The intimate depiction of historic life in *Little Syria* and its parallels to contemporary life allows Offendum to show how Arabs are woven into American cultural life. By bringing cultural objects into conversation, Offendum creates a space to learn about cultural continuity and find spaces to create harmonies in our own lives.

NOTES
1. See, for example, a playbill for a performance of *Romeo and Juliet* put on by the Syrian American Club of New York in 1910, which can be found in Brooklyn Academy of Music's online archives.
2. Chaudhary, "Hakawati."

REFERENCES
Chaudhary, Suchitra Bajpai. "Hakawati: The Ancient Arab Art of Storytelling." Arts Culture – Gulf News. Gulf News, May 25, 2019. https://gulfnews.com

/entertainment/arts-culture/hakawati-the-ancient-arab-art-of-storytelling-1.712001.

Jacobs, Linda K. *Strangers in the West: The Syrian Colony of New York City, 1880–1900*. New York: Kalimah Press, 2015.

"PROGRAM/PLAYBILL ROMEO AND JULIET." Shelby White & Leon Levy BAM digital archive: Promotional: Romeo and Juliet [1910.00032]. BAM Hamm Archives. Accessed August 22, 2022. https://levyarchive.bam.org/Detail/objects/4643.

REVIEWED BY IRINA SHEYNFELD

RAFAEL LOZANO-HEMMER
Drawings in Smoke

> "I grew up in Mexico City with parents who were nightclub owners and the artificial lights, strobes, disco balls—all of this is part of how I grew up. Most of the time, I think of art as a good party. You can play good music and bring in ambiance with lights but it's the people that make the party. You create a setting but it is only in the arrival of the people that the participation of the piece comes alive. "[1]
> —Rafael Lozano-Hemmer

Rafael Lozano-Hemmer (b.1967) is a Mexican-Canadian artist known for his monumental participatory projects that involve proprietary technology and often deal with political themes of globalization, surveillance, and government control. While the artist's work is often politically and socially attuned, Lozano's solo exhibition *Common Measures* (on view at Pace in New York City in the fall of 2022) was more than a didactic lecture on the postindustrial human condition. Three works in the exhibition—*Pulse Topology* (2021), *Call on Water* (2016), and *Hormonium* (2022)—were mesmerizing, thought provoking, deeply spiritual, and personal. In his latest work, Lozano-Hemmer surpasses the practice of social commentary and crosses over into the phantasmagoric and magical realm of art that deals with themes of mortality, vanishing poetry, and disappearing archives. (See figure 1.)

Lozano-Hemmer started to create installations of *Pulse* in 2006, and the first *Pulse* work made its debut at Plataforma, Fábrica La Constancia in Puebla, Mexico. The centerpiece of *Common Measures* is an immersive, biometric artwork, *Pulse Topology*. It consists of three thousand light bulbs suspended from the ceiling to create an inverse topographical model. The network of lightbulbs forms hills and valleys of light above visitors' heads. The darkness of the gallery is illuminated by the pulsating world above and the artwork shimmers like a city viewed from an airplane, except that the relationship to the viewer is inverted. The flickering pattern of civilization is above our heads and we move below,

Figure 1. Rafael Lozano-Hemmer *Pulse Topology*, 2021 3000 LED filament lightbulbs, DMX controllers, custom-made photoplethysmography sensors, computers covers any area between 1,000 and 5,000 square feet.

under its luminous and delicate mantle. The viewer feels small, alone, and disconnected in Lozano's upside down forest of electric fireflies.

The latest *Pulse* installation is a large-scale and immersive work in the tradition of Mexican muralists such as Diego Rivera and Jose Clemente Orozco. Similar to his predecessors, many of Lozano-Hemmer's pieces, such as *Voz Alta* (2008), deal with violent chapters of recent Mexican history. *Voz Alta* is a commentary on a bloody massacre that occurred on October 2, 1968, when Mexican Armed Forces opened fire on a peaceful rally, killing several hundred people. Yet, *Pulse* is different from other works in the artist's practice. It remains politically neutral and deals with timeless questions of life, death, and time. Also, unlike Rivera's and Orozco's murals, which were meant to appeal to the masses, in *Pulse*, Lozano-Hemmer's work becomes personal, intimate, and poetic, even though many people can view it at the same time.

The lights in *Pulse Topology* react to sensors that record new visitors' heartbeats. Each newcomer is assigned a light bulb. The digital traces of visitors' presence linger for a while, creating a temporary visual archive of gallery goers coming and going as well as commenting on their short life spans. In their chapter from *Rafael Lozano-Hemmer: Unstable*

Presence, "Pulse on Pulse: Modulation and Signification," Merete Carlson and Ulrik Schmidt write,

> The visitor's relation to the work . . . begins as an encounter with the sculpture as physical structure (object), but evolves into a complex subject-interface situation, in which the visitor animates the light bulb and faces a visual representation of their pulse. This representation is heavily loaded with symbolic meaning: what you see in front of you is a copy of your own pulsating heart. [2]

The light bulb becomes you for a while until you are replaced with a representation of another visitor's heartbeat. The flickering electric light is a trace of you that doesn't last forever in the world and that reminds one of their mortality, or *memento mori*. Memento mori—"remember that you must die"—is a recurring theme in Western art. The term comes from the Book of Ecclesiastes: "One generation passeth away, and another generation cometh: but the earth abideth for ever."[3] We burn as bright as Lozano's bulbs and then we disappear into the night, making room for the new light to take our place.

In the next room at Pace, we find two more works by the artist: *Call on Water* (2016), and *Hormonium* (2022). *Call on Water* is a fountain in the shape of a rectangular basin that has misty occult-looking white vapors steaming out of its depths. The gallery is dark with a spotlight shining bluish white light onto the mass of steam that rises from the fountain's basin. With the vapors, the work spells out words from Mexican poet Octavio Paz's poems; Paz was also Lozano-Hemmer's uncle. In an interview with VICE News's *The Creators Project*, Lozano-Hemmer explained,

> The whole piece is an homage to Octavio Paz, a very influential writer in general, but also for me in particular as he was my uncle from my father's side. I wanted to see his words written with water vapor and erased by turbulence. His work is perfect for this ephemeral writing machine that turns poems into atmospheric phenomena that can be breathed in.[4]

The viewer cannot really read or understand sentences that the fountain releases into the atmosphere. Instead, one gets an almost sublime feeling of mystery and communication with forces beyond the material world.

Like *Pulse*, *Call on Water* is a personal and poetic work that seems to communicate with each viewer individually, and like *Pulse*, it explores the idea of traces that one can leave in this world or not. Its milky gray

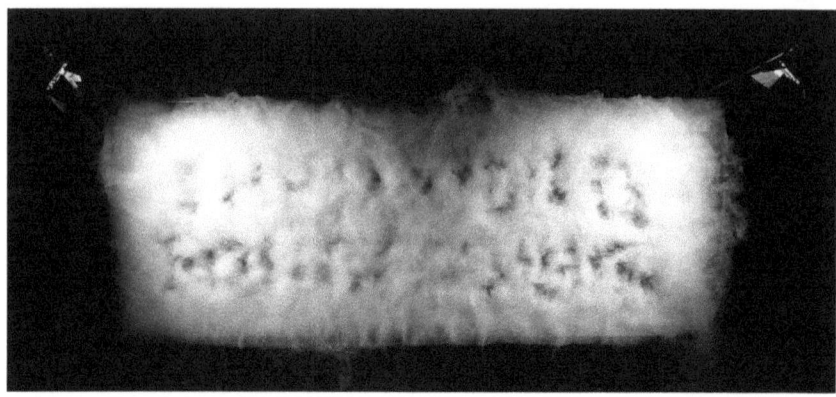

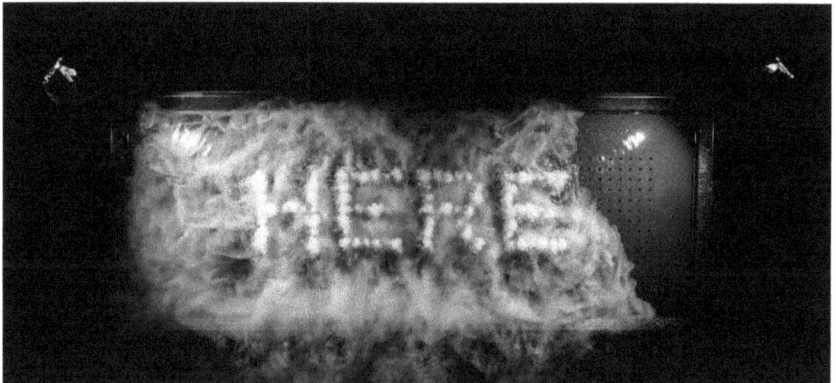

Figures 2 and 3. Rafael Lozano-Hemmer *Call on Water*, 2016. Ultrasonic atomizers, aluminum and steel basin, custom electronics, computer, waterdistiller.116-1/8" × 44-7/8" × 13-3/4" (295 cm × 114 cm × 34.9 cm)

vapors swirl around the black rectangular basin as if alive and waiting for you to come closer and decipher its messages. The work spells words and phrases using hundreds of computer-controlled ultrasonic atomizers.[5] When plumes of cold, smoky vapor come up from the basin's depth, there is something magical about the way they materialize and vanish without leaving any tangible trace. The fountain breathes poetry; it is alive, and although it is hard to discern its message, we are drawn to it because it appears to be speaking directly to each of us.

Across the room from *Call on Water*, one encounters a large monitor with a continuous video of black and white waves—*Hormonium*. It is a generative artwork that represents all the hormones of the human body. In an interview with VernissageTV, Lozano-Hemmer explains that his

Figure 4. Rafael Lozano-Hemmer *Hormonium*, 2022 custom-generative code, computer, display Variable, 4K, 75" or 85" flat screen

team worked closely with an endocrinologist who helped them understand how hormones control and modulate our bodies throughout the day, and throughout our lives—our age. *Hormonium*'s software generates life cycles that evoke those of a human being. If one looks closer at the ocean waves crashing over an invisible shore, it is possible to discern acronyms that represent hormones that people release throughout their lives. For example, TSH is a thyroid hormone, and GH is a growth hormone. This meditative work is an attempt to understand systems that control the chaos of our lives—systems that sustain and generate themselves without our knowledge and despite our unawareness. They are as natural and constant as the ocean or anything else that moves and evolves and vanishes without a trace in our world.

All three works in *Common Measures* deal with themes of mortality, fragility, and ephemeral beauty. What are we, his works seem to ask, but light bulbs that are ready to go out? What is it that we create? None of it is more permanent than drawings made by the waves of the receding surf, the flickering pattern of electric lights, or words formed by smoke, mirrors, and breath.

NOTES

1. Lozano-Hemmer, "Pulse Topology."
2. Carlson and Schmidt, "Pulse on Pulse," 130.

3. Eccles. 1:4 (King James Version)
4. Campuzano, "Animated Vapor Art."
5. "Call on Water."

REFERENCES

"Call on Water." Rafael Lozano-Hemmer. Accessed December 5, 2022. https://www.lozano-hemmer.com/call_on_water.php.

Campuzano, Rodrigo. "Animated Vapor Art Writes a Poem in Thin Air." *The Creators Project* (blog), VICE News, August 16, 2016. https://www.vice.com/en/article/yp597w/vapor-made-poetry-art-fountain.

Frieling, Rudolf, and François LeTourneux, eds. *Rafael Lozano-Hemmer: Unstable Presence*. San Francisco: San Francisco Museum of Modern Art, 2020.

Lozano-Hemmer, "Pulse Topology: A Conversation with Artist Rafael Lozano-Hemmer." By Grace Pritchett. MIKCexplore, November 8, 2021. https://mikcexplore.com/home/2021/11/8/pulse-topology-a-conversation-with-artist-rafael-lozano-hemmer.

"Pulse Room." Rafael Lozano-Hemmer. Accessed October 24, 2022. https://www.lozano-hemmer.com/pulse_room.php.

"Relational Aesthetics." Tate. Accessed October 24, 2022. https://www.tate.org.uk/art/art-terms/r/relational-aesthetics.

Schmidt, Ulrik, and Merete Carlson. "Pulse on Pulse: Modulation and Signification." In *Rafael Lozano-Hemmer: Unstable Presence*, edited by Rudolf Frieling and François LeTourneux, 129–31. San Francisco: San Francisco Museum of Modern Art, 2020.

VernissageTV. "Rafael Lozano-Hemmer: Excuse You! Solo Exhibition at Wilde Gallery Basel." YouTube. YouTube, June 26, 2022. https://www.youtube.com/watch?v=dQ3dSjyJHrg.

IRINA SHEYNFELD

IMPOSSIBLE VOYAGES
Wangechi Mutu at Storm King

> "My work is for my daughters and my sons and the next generation who will hopefully continue to create new ways of telling our histories and of stitching us all back together."[1]
> —Wangechi Mutu

Kenyan-born American multidisciplinary visual artist Wangechi Mutu (b. 1972) brings her fantastical menagerie of beings to the expansive landscape of Storm King Art Center, an open-air museum about ninety miles north of New York City. The artist divides her time in the studio between Nairobi and New York City and in her practice, she incorporates elements from both worlds. Her work has been described as deeply feminist and informed by both Afrofuturism—a cultural aesthetic that combines science fiction, history, and fantasy to explore the African American experience—and Symbiocene, a term coined in 2011 by Glen Albrecht, that describes a new era in human history that is characterized by harmonious interactions between humans and all other living beings. Eight large-scale sculptures populate the museum hill and about twenty additional works, including two films, span two floors of the main museum building. This is perhaps one of the artist's most comprehensive solo shows to date.

Mutu's work is an intervention into Storm King's pastoral, hilly landscape and it encourages a conversation between museums past and present. It also makes us think anew about the importance of ritual and its creation, as well as the new meaning of one's journey through life. In her practice, Mutu doesn't just rethink existing mythologies but she often creates new ones. She conjures fantastical, futuristic female beings and creates worlds for them to travel through. Mutu deals with themes of reinventing the journey, rewriting mythology, and reconstructing ritual. The artist creates new creatures on a voyage through unknown territory. Both of her most recent sculptural groups, *In Two Canoe* (2022) and *Crocodylus* (2020), depict travelers whose destination and purpose are

Figure 1. *In Two Canoe*, 2022 Bronze 180 x 68 x 72 in (457.2 x 172.7 x 182.9 cm) Edition 1/3

unknown, while *Shavasana I* and *II* (2019) present us with those whose journey has just ended.

On top of Museum Hill, at the center of the park and right in front of the museum building, there is a fifteen-foot-long bronze fountain, *In Two Canoe*. It consists of two patinated olive-green humanoid female figures seated inside a water-filled boat. Both women's legs are spread wide and hang down over the sides of the canoe into the earth as slender mangrove roots. In an interview with the *New York Times*, Mutu explains that, "Mangroves are migratory. This plant has moved everywhere and has made journeys like those who were kidnapped from Africa and taken to the Americas. The water seals this unified story we've created for ourselves. We are all connected on this sphere of earth and the water is how we go and find each other." But where are two giantesses going in a boat that is filled to the brim with water? The unexpected placement of the water—inside rather than outside of the boat—makes one wonder how these woodland leaf-covered aliens are going to get anywhere. Does it mean that their mysterious journey is doomed from the get-go?

Mutu's beings are simultaneously awe- and fear-inspiring. The couple in *Canoe* recalls a small stone plaque from the mid-fourteenth century

Figure 2. *In Two Canoe*, 2022 Bronze 180 x 68 x 72 in (457.2 x 172.7 x 182.9 cm) Edition 1/3

BCE, *Akhenaten, Nefertiti and Their Three Daughters Under the Strahlenaton*. The stele, which is housed at the Neues Museum in Berlin, is unique in the three-thousand-year history of Egyptian Art, as it depicts Pharaoh and his wife not idealized in a canonical way but as equals seated in front of each other.[2] One notices a striking resemblance between the figures of Mutu's *Canoe* and those depicted on the *Akhenaten* plaque; they share elongated heads and their necks and limbs are exaggerated, as if they have been stretched. Like Mutu's beings, Akhenaten and Nefertiti project familial warmth even as their anatomy conjures otherness. Their bodies are defined with flowing lines that Mutu also favors. They are shown on the same scale, seated on similar chairs—a composition that suggests the possibility of the king and queen having ruled Egypt together. In Mutu's sculpture, blindfolded figures face each other in the same manner. Thus, this twenty-first-century artist engages in a conversation with ancient Egyptian art and, at the same time, creates a link between her work and the origins of both African and Western art. While writing her chapter in this new interwoven history, she foregrounds a woman traveler, searcher, and explorer as the protagonist of her story.

Not far from *In Two Canoe* on Museum Hill one finds *Crocodylus,* a highly stylized sculptural group that consists of a female rider seated on top of a giant, larger-than-life crocodile. The connection between this sculpture and myths and legends, as well as the reality, surrounding life near the Nile is uncanny. In ancient Egypt, the crocodile was feared and mythologized as a powerful water creature who still claims about one thousand lives every year in places where large crocodilians are native.[3] Thousands of mummified crocodiles were found in a vast crocodile necropolis in the Egyptian town of Tebtunis. The crocodile god Sobek was associated with the fertility that the river Nile would bring with its flooding waters. Nile crocodiles can grow to over twenty feet in length and weigh more than 1,000 pounds.[4] It is not surprising that Mutu chose such a ferocious, fertile, and powerful animal as a mode of transportation and a companion for her rider.

Crocodiles' most common victims were and probably still are among the most vulnerable members of a society: women who come to wash clothes on the river bank and children who tag along. Perhaps Mutu's *Crocodylus* is their protector and avatar. Artist and art historian Claudia Schmuckli points out that "Mutu resurrects these [Egyptian] legends into a hybrid creature that invokes legions of fantastical avengers but also reworks the representation of the Hindu deity Ganga riding a Makara (Sanskrit for sea dragon or water monster) into a contemporary fighter figure."[5] The *Crocodylus* rider is situated low to the ground. She holds the beast with her strong legs; her entire body ripples with musculature. The rider commands the animal, but she is also united

Figure 3. *Crocodylus*, 2020 Bronze 167 x 87 x 73 in. (424.18 x 220.98 x 185.42 cm) Edition 1/3

with it through shared texture and line patterns. Is the mysterious rider about to destroy serpents hidden in bronze baskets that are scattered around the Storm King grounds, or is she about to venture on the quest to save disempowered victims, such as the subjects of *Shavasana I* and *II*, another sculptural group of two African American women, lying lifeless under yoga mats?

We do not see the faces of *Shavasana I* and *II* figures: their arms and legs are spread-eagle on the ground. The artist gives them neither pedestals nor glory to reflect their low stature today's society. Here Mutu neither sexualizes, idealizes, nor elevates her subjects. The viewer's eye is drawn to their vulnerable pink toenails and matching high-heeled shoes, the only worldly possessions that identify them as women. Their lifeless bodies attract and resist the viewer's gaze. Who killed these two? What happened here? Raw pain of the recent death emanates from the sculpture. In an interview with Claudia Schmuckli, Mutu explained that as she was working on the *Shavasana* pieces, Nia Wilson's murder was in the news:

Figure 4. *Shavasana II*, 2019 Bronze 83 x 53 x 9 1/2 in. (210.8 x 134.6 x 24.1 cm) Edition 1/3

She was so young, and they kept showing her picture before she died. Her father went to the area where she was killed, and they had put a tarp on top of her . . . It struck me so deeply because I remember thinking, What would I do if I showed up somewhere and someone said, "That's one of your daughters under there"? I mean how do you even pick up that tarp to look and see what's under there.[6]

Perhaps the *Shavasana* sculptural duet represents victims that the crocodile rider sets out to protect, or the fate that the two in the Canoe seek to escape. Whether destroyers or redeemers, Mutu's women are unleashed on our world—conquering and remaking its story as they progress on their journey.

NOTES
1. Mutu, "I Am Speaking," 49.
2. "Akhenaten, Nefertiti, and Three Daughters."
3. "What Are the World's Deadliest Animals?"
4. Ruane, "Crocodiles Were so Revered in Ancient Egypt That They Were Hunted, Killed and Mummified."

5. Schmuckli, "Art as a 'Weapon of Mass Construction,'" 25.
6. Schmuckli et al., "Making Histories," 47.

REFERENCES

"Afrofuturism." Tate. Accessed September 10, 2022. https://www.tate.org.uk/art/art-terms/a/afrofuturism.

"Akhenaten, Nefertiti, and Three Daughters." Smarthistory, July 29, 2012. https://youtu.be/ryycDVWXDvc.

Mutu, Wangechi. "I Am Speaking." In *Wangechi Mutu: I Am Speaking, Are You Listening?*, by Claudia Schmuckli, Wangechi Mutu, and Isaac Julien, 48–50. San Francisco: Fine Arts Museums of San Francisco, 2021.

Ruane, Michael E. "Crocodiles Were so Revered in Ancient Egypt That They Were Hunted, Killed and Mummified." *Washington Post*, October 17, 2019. https://www.washingtonpost.com/history/2019/09/20/crocodiles-were-so-revered-ancient-egypt-that-they-were-hunted-killed-mummified/.

Schmuckli, Claudia. "Art as a 'Weapon of Mass Construction.'" In *Wangechi Mutu: I Am Speaking, Are You Listening?*, by Claudia Schmuckli, Wangechi Mutu, and Isaac Julien 16–36. San Francisco: Fine Arts Museums of San Francisco, 2021.

Schmuckli, Claudia, Isaac Julien, and Wangechi Mutu. "Making Histories: Wangechi Mutu in Conversation with Isaac Julien and Claudia Schmuckli." In *Wangechi Mutu: I Am Speaking, Are You Listening?*, by Claudia Schmuckli, Wangechi Mutu, and Isaac Julien, 36–47. San Francisco: Fine Arts Museums of San Francisco, 2021.

"What Are the World's Deadliest Animals?" BBC News, June 15, 2016. https://www.bbc.com/news/world-36320744.

CONTRIBUTORS

Domenik Ackermann studied Protestant Theology in Göttingen (Germany), Heidelberg (Germany), and Beirut (Lebanon) with a focus on ecumenical issues and interfaith questions. A Ph. D. Candidate at the Theology Department at Boston College, his research interests include comparative theological and liturgical studies on Christianity and Judaism with a particular emphasis on the function of memory in prayerful activity. His dissertation "Prayerful Memory. What Christian Theology Can Learn from Jewish Practice" explores the meaning of prayer as an experience through Jean-Louis-Chrétien and Johann Baptist Metz in dialogue with Jewish liturgical functions of prayer. Domenik is an ordained minister in the United Church of Christ (UCC).

Shannon Hardwick's work has appeared, or is forthcoming, in *Gulf Coast Journal*, *The Texas Observer*, *The Missouri Review*, *Four Way Review*, *Salamander*, *Sixth Finch*, and *Passages North*, among others. Hardwick serves as the Editor-in-Chief at *The Boiler Journal*.

Paul Hedges is Associate Professor in the SRP Programme, RSIS, Nanyang Technological University, Singapore. He has published fourteen books (most recently *Understanding Religion* and *Religious Hatred*) and over seventy academic papers.

Aya Nimer is a Program Manager at Pillars Fund, where she works on developing culture change programming that advances Pillars' mission of changing narratives around Muslims in the U.S. Her programmatic work builds on interdisciplinary artistic and scholarly approaches to care, community building, and culture change. Aya earned her bachelor's degree from The University of Chicago in an interdisciplinary program focused on social theory in philosophy and allied fields. She holds a master's degree in Humanities with a concentration in the Social History of Art from The University of Chicago.

Hesron H. Sihombing is a doctoral student at the University of Denver/Iliff School of Theology in Denver, USA. His academic interest lies at the intersection of public theology, postcolonial/decolonial studies, and economic/ecological ethics. Sihombing is an ordained minister at the *Gereja Kristen Protestan Indonesia* (Indonesia) and belongs to the Batak ethnic group.

Michelle Voss Roberts is professor of theology and past principal at Emmanuel College in the Toronto School of Theology. She has authored three book-length works of comparative theology on Christian and Hindu traditions. She is also the editor of a volume that brings interreligious comparison to the introductory study of theology, *Comparative Theology: Insights for Systematic Theological Reflection* (Fordham University Press, 2016), and co-editor of the *Routledge Handbook of Hindu-Christian Relations* (Routledge Press, 2020).

Irina Sheynfeld is a freelance art historian, painter, and graphic designer. She was born in Odessa, Ukraine where she was trained as a puppet-maker and fine artist. Now, Irina lives and works in New York City with her three sons and a miniature labradoodle, Luke Skywalker.

O'neil Van Horn is Teaching Professor of Theology at Xavier University in Cincinnati, OH and is a Louisville Scholar (2021–2023). He holds a PhD in Philosophical and Theological Studies from Drew University and specializes in the intersections between constructive theology, critical theory, and environmental justice. He has published various articles and book chapters in the fields of theopoetics, constructive ecotheology, and environmental philosophy. He is the author of the forthcoming book, *On the Ground: Terrestrial Theopoetics and Planetary Politics for the Anthropocene* (2023).

www.ingramcontent.com/pod-product-compliance
Lightning Source LLC
Chambersburg PA
CBHW040300170426
43193CB00020B/2958